Eyes
on
Spies

The Hoover Institution gratefully acknowledges
the following individuals and foundations
for their significant support of the

HOOVER
INSTITUTION
STANFORD
UNIVERSITY

KORET-TAUBE TASK FORCE
ON NATIONAL SECURITY AND LAW

Koret Foundation

Tad and Dianne Taube
  Taube Family Foundation

James J. Carroll III
  Jean Perkins Foundation

Eyes on Spies

Congress and
the United States
Intelligence Community

by Amy B. Zegart

HOOVER INSTITUTION PRESS
STANFORD UNIVERSITY | STANFORD, CALIFORNIA

*The Hoover Institution on War, Revolution and Peace, founded
at Stanford University in 1919 by Herbert Hoover, who went on
to become the thirty-first president of the United States, is an
interdisciplinary research center for advanced study on domestic
and international affairs. The views expressed in its publications are
entirely those of the authors and do not necessarily reflect the views
of the staff, officers, or Board of Overseers of the Hoover Institution.*

www.hoover.org

Hoover Institution Press Publication No. 603

Hoover Institution at Leland Stanford Junior University,
Stanford, California, 94305-6010

First printing 2011
17 16 15 14 13 12 11   9 8 7 6 5 4 3 2 1

Manufactured in the United States of America

The paper used in this publication meets the minimum
Requirements of the American National Standard for
Information Sciences—Permanence of Paper for Printed
Library Materials, ANSI/NISO Z39.48-1992. ∞

Library of Congress Cataloging-in-Publication Data
Zegart, Amy B., 1967–
Eyes on spies : Congress and the United States intelligence
community / by Amy B. Zegart.
    p.   cm. — (Hoover Institution Press publication ; no. 603)
Includes bibliographical references and index.
ISBN 978-0-8179-1284-0 (cloth : alk. paper) —
ISBN 978-0-8179-1286-4 (e-book)
1. Intelligence service—United States. 2. Legislative oversight—
United States. I. Title.
JK468.I6Z415 2011
155.4'124—dc23   2011031443

For Craig

CONTENTS

LIST OF TABLES AND FIGURES

ACKNOWLEDGMENTS

THE SEED OF THIS BOOK WAS PLANTED IN 2007, when the Senate Select Committee on Intelligence invited me to testify about weaknesses in intelligence oversight. It was an unusual effort by a congressional committee to examine its own flaws publicly, with the aim of generating both ideas and momentum for reform. I would like to thank Chairman John D. Rockefeller, IV (D-WV), Vice Chairman Christopher "Kit" Bond (R-MO), members of the committee, and Ken Johnson and the rest of the committee staff for tackling these issues head-on and pushing me to think about them more. Four years later, I still have oversight on the brain.

I am indebted to John Raisian, David Brady, and Peter Berkowitz for inviting me to present the first parts of this project to the Koret-Taube Task Force on National Security and Law at the Hoover Institution and for making this book possible. Thanks also to task force members Ken Anderson, Philip Bobbitt, Jack Goldsmith, Steve Krasner, Jessica Stern, Matthew Waxman, and Ben Wittes; and Joel Aberbach, E. Scott Adler, Matt Baum, Al Carnesale, Bobby Chesney, Fred Kaiser, Mark Kleiman, Kris Kasianovitz, David Mayhew, Eric Patashnik, Mark Peterson, Kal Raustiala, Andy Sabl, and Steve Teles for data suggestions and comments on earlier drafts. The improvements are theirs, but any remaining errors are all mine.

Without a small army of research assistants, I would still be analyzing twenty-five thousand interest groups and thirty years of congressional hearings. Thanks to Matt Clawson, Ravi Doshi, Katie Frost, Torey McMurdo, Greg Midgette, Jaclyn Nelson, Russell Wald, Alec Wilson, and especially Melinda McVay, who spent far more time mastering the intricacies of congressional data coding than any human being should. Thanks also to Julie Quinn for managing the army and co-authoring chapter 4, and to UCLA's Burkle Center for International Relations and the Center for American Politics and Public Policy for providing seed funding.

In the course of this and other intelligence projects, I have interviewed more than eighty intelligence officials, legislators, and staff. Most have asked to remain anonymous so that they could speak more freely. I am indebted to them all.

Thanks to my children—Kate, Jack, and Alexander—for launching the best covert operation imaginable: sneaking into my office every day after school (from different directions, seemingly undetected by the babysitter) to chat about their days. I am grateful to my parents, Shelly and Kenny Zegart, for their steadfast support through three cities, kids, and books. Thanks also to my grandfather, Judge David Weiss, who knew firsthand the joys and challenges of electoral politics and defied all of my theoretical predictions, serving in the arena with an abiding commitment to the public good. My grandmother, Thelma Weiss, passed away just as this book was going to press, but I smile knowing that she would have said she loved it, regardless of what I actually wrote.

Last but not least, this book is dedicated to my husband, Craig Mallery. For everything.

AMY B. ZEGART
September 2011

Eyes
on
Spies

CHAPTER ONE

Introduction

Ten years after 9/11, the least reformed part of America's intelligence system is not the Central Intelligence Agency (CIA) or the Federal Bureau of Investigation (FBI), but the United States Congress. The September 11th terrorist attacks sparked major efforts to transform executive branch intelligence agencies. These include the creation of the Office of the Director of National Intelligence (ODNI), the most sweeping intelligence restructuring since the establishment of the CIA in 1947; the formation of the Department of Homeland Security (DHS), which combined twenty-two agencies and two hundred thousand employees to provide "one face at the border;" dramatic initiatives to transform the FBI from a law enforcement to domestic intelligence agency; and the proliferation of more than seventy regional, state, and local fusion centers to integrate terrorist threat reporting across the country.

Although reforms have generated some major successes—including the May 2011 capture and killing of Osama bin Laden—not all intelligence improvement efforts have actually produced improvements.[1] Some reforms have failed. Many have not gone

---

1. For more on barriers to adaptation in U.S. intelligence agencies, see Amy B. Zegart, *Spying Blind: The CIA, the FBI, and the Origins of 9/11* (Princeton: Princeton University Press, 2007).

far enough, fast enough. Others have proven counterproductive, creating more red tape and fatigue than results. Recent terrorist plots, including the 2009 Fort Hood shootings, the 2009 Christmas Day underwear bomber, and the May 2010 Times Square car bomb plot, remind us all too well that serious weaknesses in the American intelligence system remain. Indeed, the confessed Times Square bomb "mastermind," Pakistani-American Faisal Shahzad, was too dumb or too poorly trained to construct a workable explosive or park his car bomb inconspicuously (he abandoned his Nissan Pathfinder with its engine running and hazard lights flashing, which immediately attracted the attention of nearby street vendors). Yet Shahzad still managed to outsmart his FBI surveillance team, losing them somewhere between Connecticut and John F. Kennedy International Airport in New York. And despite being placed on the "no-fly list," he was able to board a Dubai-bound flight and was just minutes from takeoff when Customs and Border Patrol agents realized he was on board and apprehended him. Shahzad later pleaded guilty to all ten terrorism-related charges against him.

Despite this record, it is clear that the seventeen agencies that comprise the United States Intelligence Community are expending considerable energy attempting to adapt to ever-changing terrorist threats.[2] As one senior FBI official put it, "This is all I do,

---

2. The term "Intelligence Community" or "IC" is widely used to describe the constellation of federal government agencies that collect and analyze intelligence. (In addition, a growing number of states, cities, counties, and regions are developing their own intelligence analysis and coordination capabilities.) The size and cohesion of the Intelligence Community have varied over time. Before 9/11, the IC consisted of a dozen agencies that acted more like warring tribes than elements of a coherent system. Since 9/11 the IC has grown to seventeen agencies which are more cohesive but still struggling to work in a unified fashion. The IC currently consists of: The Office of the Director of National Intelligence; the Central Intelligence Agency; eight Defense Department intelligence agencies (the Defense Intelligence Agency, the National Geospatial Intelligence Agency, the National Reconnaissance Office, the National Security Agency, and intelligence units in the

okay? 24/7, 365 days a year. I don't have a wife. I don't have kids. It's all I think about."[3] The same is true in the field. "The burn out rate in my Al Qaeda squad is terrible," noted one FBI agent in May 2010. "And these are agents who have done other CT [counterterrorism] work, where the pace is already tough. They're just getting crushed by the load."[4] Just above the doorway that leads to the CIA's Counterterrorism Center hangs a sign that reads, "Today's date is September 12, 2001." Spend any amount of time there, or in a military unit in Afghanistan, the New York Police Department, the Office of the Director of National Intelligence, or any of the other federal intelligence agencies charged with collecting and analyzing intelligence, and you will quickly realize just how many people are working feverishly to adapt to what they call, simply, "the mission."

Congress is another story. While Congress has been instrumental in many post-9/11 executive branch reforms, Congress has been largely unable to reform itself. In 2004, the 9/11 Commission called congressional oversight "dysfunctional," and warned that fixing oversight weaknesses would be both essential to American national security and exceedingly difficult to achieve.[5] One

---

Army, Navy, Air Force, and Marines); two intelligence agencies in the Department of Justice (the FBI and the Drug Enforcement Agency); two units in the Department of Homeland Security (the U.S. Coast Guard and the Office of Intelligence and Analysis); the Department of Energy's Office of Intelligence and Counterintelligence; the Department of State's Bureau of Intelligence and Research; and the Treasury Department's Office of Intelligence and Analysis. For more about the organization and functions of IC component elements, see Office of the Director of National Intelligence, *National Intelligence: A Consumer's Guide*, available at http://www.dni.gov/IC_Consumers_Guide_2009.pdf (March 2010) and Office of the Director of National Intelligence, *An Overview of the United States Intelligence Community for the 111*th *Congress*, available at http://www.dni.gov/overview.pdg (July 2010).

3. Interview by author, 9 February 2007.
4. Interview by author, 12 May 2010.
5. *The 9/11 Commission Report: Final Report of the National Commission on Terrorist Attacks upon the United States* (New York: W.W. Norton, 2004), pp. 419–423.

year later, the Commission's report card gave efforts to improve intelligence oversight a "D."[6] That same year, a second blue-ribbon commission (chaired by Judge Laurence Silberman and former Senator Chuck Robb), which was tasked with examining what went wrong with estimates of Iraqi weapons of mass destruction (WMD), joined the call for oversight reform. That commission's final report concluded that "Many sound past proposals for intelligence reform have withered on the vine. Either the Intelligence Community is inherently resistant to outside recommendations, or it lacks the institutional capacity to implement them. *In either case, sustained external oversight is necessary*" (emphasis mine).[7] Although many of the Silberman-Robb Commission's executive branch reforms were adopted, its congressional reforms were not embraced.

By the fall of 2007, the Senate Select Committee on Intelligence grew so deeply concerned that it held a hearing on itself. I testified at that hearing, along with Lee Hamilton, who served as the 9/11 Commission's vice chairman and earlier as chairman of the House Permanent Select Committee on Intelligence (HPSCI). Pointing his finger at all the senators around the room, Hamilton delivered an ominous warning:

> To me, the strong point simply is that the Senate of the United States and the House of the United States is [sic] not doing its job. And because you're not doing the job, the country is not as safe as it ought to be. . . . You're dealing here with the national security of the United States, and the Senate and the House

6. 9/11 Commission Public Discourse Project, *Final Report on 9/11 Commission Recommendations*, 5 December 2005, accessed at http://www.9/11-pdp.org (4 August 2009).

7. The Commission on the Intelligence Capabilities of the United States Regarding Weapons of Mass Destruction (WMD Commission), *Final Report of the Commission on The Intelligence Capabilities of the United States Regarding Weapons of Mass Destruction* (31 March 2005), p. 20. Accessed at http://govinfo.library.unt.edu/wmd/report/wmd_report.pdf (7 July 2010).

ought to have the deep down feeling that we've got to get this
thing right.[8]

Hamilton's words prompted vigorous nods of agreement across
the aisle, but never made headlines or produced major changes.[9]
Instead, the committee's own oversight-reform centerpiece—
consolidating appropriations and authorization powers—quickly
and quietly died. In May 2009, House Speaker Nancy Pelosi
(D-CA) declared in a press conference that oversight had become
so feckless, the only way to change Bush administration intelligence
policies was to oust Republicans at the polls.[10] And in January
2010, eight years after 9/11, a third blue-ribbon commission—the
Commission on the Prevention of Weapons of Mass Destruction
Proliferation and Terrorism—concluded that congressional intelligence and homeland security reform efforts were still failing.
Notably, nearly all of the proposed oversight changes required simply modifying internal congressional rules and committee jurisdictions, not passing new laws.[11]

This book examines the roots of weak intelligence oversight and
why deficiencies have persisted for so long, despite the clarion call
for change after 9/11 and the unprecedented importance of intelligence in today's threat environment. As many have noted, during the Cold War the Soviet adversary was easy to find but hard

8. Senate Select Committee on Intelligence (SSCI), Hearing on Congressional
Oversight, 110th Cong., 1st sess., 13 November 2007.

9. Hamilton's testimony was not covered in any major U.S. newspapers, radio, or television broadcasts. LexisNexis search from hearing date of 13 November 2007 to 11 December 2007, conducted 11 June 2009.

10. Transcript of Nancy Pelosi 14 May 2009 press conference. Accessed at
http://www.washingtonpost.com/wp-dyn/content/article/2009/05/14/AR2009
051402100.html (30 July 2009).

11. Commission on the Prevention of Weapons of Mass Destruction Proliferation and Terrorism, *Report Card*, 26 January 2010, 12. Accessed at http://www
.preventwmd.gov/about/ (4 May 2010). Although Congress later that year managed to pass an intelligence authorization bill for the first time since 2004, several
key oversight measures were stripped or watered down.

to kill, making military firepower the key to success. Today, the situation is reversed; our terrorist enemies are hard to find but easy to kill. It is now the weak who threaten the strong. Driven by fanaticism, hidden from view, and armed with Internet connections and deadly weapons that can fit into a suitcase or vial, small bands of transnational terrorists can wreak catastrophic damage as never before. In the twenty-first century threat environment, intelligence has eclipsed military firepower as the nation's most important line of defense. Nowhere was the importance of intelligence more prominent than in the May 1, 2011 operation to kill Osama bin Laden at his Pakistani hideout. Success required no tanks, massive aerial bombardment, or invasion. The "boots on the ground" did not number in the hundreds of thousands, or even the hundreds. Instead, the operation to nab the world's most dangerous terrorist came down to just two critical elements: a small, elite Navy SEAL team and actionable intelligence that had been painstakingly collected and analyzed over a period of years.

Intelligence agencies cannot go it alone. Legislative oversight, done well, ensures that the Intelligence Community gets the resources it needs and deploys those resources to maximum effect. Good oversight sets agencies' strategic priorities and pushes them to improve by asking tough questions and demanding better answers. Good oversight also maintains accountability by ensuring compliance with the law and generating public trust and support for agencies that must, by necessity, hide much of what they do.

Oversight done poorly, however, can hurt our national intelligence effort. Congressional micromanagement of intelligence activities serves no one's interests well, distracting agencies from their missions and miring legislators in the day-to-day rather than focusing attention on the bigger and more important questions of what American intelligence agencies should be doing, how well they are doing it, and where they should be heading in the future. Accountability efforts can and do often go awry, saddling intelligence officials with onerous reporting requirements that sap time and attention from their day jobs to answer queries, write letters, and produce reports that no one reads.[12] In 2009, for example, the Department of Homeland Security spent 66 work years responding to congressional questions, giving 2,058 briefings, and sending 232 witnesses to 166 hearings. "It's disgraceful," said Representative Peter King (R-NY), who chairs the House Homeland Security Committee. "There's no good reason."[13]

In addition, too often oversight consists of blaming agencies when things turn ugly and the cameras are rolling rather than partnering with them to prevent mishaps in the first place or working constructively to address weaknesses when no one is watching. Responsiveness can also be a double-edged sword, either keeping unelected intelligence officials from running amok or making them run in too many directions at once. Intelligence oversight, in short, is a critical component of national security in the twenty-first century. Getting it right is hard, and getting it wrong is dangerous.

Since 9/11, most explanations of Congress's weak intelligence oversight have blamed the executive branch. Critics have focused

12. Ogul tracked all reports sent by the executive branch to Congress during three years in the 1960s and found that not a single congressional committee had a systematic process for preserving or filing the reports it received. Perhaps more important, Ogul found that "no one reported any strong sense of deprivation because such files were not maintained." Nearly all of his interviews suggested that most reports were not, in fact, read because the press of events and demands on legislators' time were simply too great. As one legislator joked, "We have to keep the wastebaskets full to survive." Morris S. Ogul, Congress Oversees the Bureaucracy (Pittsburgh: University of Pittsburgh Press, 1976), p. 177.
13. Associated Press, "Inside Washington: For Homeland Security Department, Too Much of a Good Thing?" *Washington Post*, 17 May 2011.

particularly on the Bush administration and the extent to which officials withheld information from Congress about secret and controversial programs such as the National Security Agency's warrantless wiretapping, the CIA's use of harsh interrogation methods, and the establishment of CIA black sites to detain suspected terrorists abroad. In a particularly charged episode, House Speaker Nancy Pelosi accused the CIA in May 2009 of "misleading" Congress "all the time," both about weapons of mass destruction in Iraq and the use of waterboarding and other harsh interrogation techniques on suspected terrorists.[14] Pelosi's charges ignited a firestorm. The CIA produced records showing the Speaker had, in fact, been briefed about waterboarding and other controversial interrogation methods on 4 September 2002, and again in early 2003. The Speaker, in turn, claimed that the September briefing said the techniques were not yet being used when in fact they were.

While the Pelosi episode had a particularly partisan and political cast to it, it is important to note that many others, including Republican staffers and career intelligence officials, have acknowledged that the Intelligence Community often does not fully, proactively, or clearly disclose what it knows or does. Even after 9/11, Congress has had recurring problems gaining access to FBI documents. As one legislative staffer lamented in 2008, "Republicans and Democrats alike cannot get [FBI] reports. The silver lining with the FBI is that at least they're nonpartisan in their non-cooperation with Congress."[15] Veteran CIA clandestine operative Robert Baer noted a similar pattern with the CIA's overseers. "I used to joke that we treat Congress like mushrooms: keep them in the dark and feed them shit." But, he quickly added,

14. Transcript of Nancy Pelosi 14 May 2009 press conference. Accessed at http://www.washingtonpost.com/wp-dyn/content/article/2009/05/14/AR2009 051402100.html (30 July 2009).
15. Interview by author, 12 March 2008.

Congress also did not want to know much. "I knew [House Intelligence Committee Chairman] Goss's chief of staff, but no one ever called me," he said.[16] A former intelligence official recounted the delicate task of briefing the congressional intelligence committees—in this case, about the secret destruction of nearly a hundred videotapes showing harsh CIA interrogations of top Al Qaeda operatives Abu Zubaydah and Abd al-Rahim al-Nashiri. "I went to the Hill and told them the tapes no longer existed," the official noted. "Now, I said they no longer exist[ed]. I did not say we crushed them up. It was up to them to figure out the rest. But I did not bury it."[17]

As these examples suggest, executive branch secrecy is an important and complicated part of the oversight story. But it is by no means the only part. Congress also has struggled to bolster its own intelligence oversight capabilities for years, with limited success. Observers have been quick to examine how the executive branch has asserted broad powers and guarded information, but slow to understand why Congress has not strengthened its own oversight tools. What former Senate Intelligence Committee Chairman John D. Rockefeller, IV has called the "long and sordid history" of congressional oversight weaknesses is not widely known, even though it began before 9/11 and continues today.[18]

In the pages that follow, I argue that many of Congress's biggest oversight problems lie with Congress. Let me be clear: by Congress, I mean the institution, not the political wrangling between parties or personalities that usually makes headlines. Much has been written about party polarization and the decline of the bipartisan foreign policy consensus since the Cold War. While intelligence policymaking has undoubtedly become more partisan and

16. Interview by author, 18 November 2004.
17. Interview by author, 19 August 2009.
18. Senator Rockefeller opening statement, SSCI Hearing on Congressional Oversight, 110th Cong., 1st sess., 13 November 2007.

rancorous in recent years, and while individual personalities matter, I find that the root causes of intelligence oversight dysfunction cross party lines, presidential administrations, individual congressional leaders, and eras.[19] Simply put, Congress has *never* expended as much effort overseeing intelligence as other policy areas. Whether Democrats or Republicans controlled the House and Senate; whether government was unified (with a single party controlling the presidency and both houses of Congress) or divided between parties; whether a committee was run by a charismatic chair or a weak one; or whether parties were more or less polarized from each other has never mattered as much as we think. Indeed, party ideology scores show quite clearly that congressional intelligence committee members have *not* been drawn from the extreme wings of the Democrat and Republican parties for the past twenty years. Instead, as I discuss more fully in chapter 2, the intelligence committees have been populated by legislators who are typically more moderate than their party colleagues in the House and Senate.

The sources of intelligence oversight deficiencies go deeper. They rest in the electoral incentives that drive all legislators—from liberal Democrats to conservative Republicans—to behave in the ways they do, and committee turf battles that almost always protect the status quo. The real story here is not about personalities, political animus, or ideological conflict. It is about how Congress has collectively and persistently tied its own hands in intelligence oversight for a very long time.

Two institutional weaknesses are paramount: rules, procedures, and practices that have hindered the development of *legislative*

---

19. For increasing partisanship in intelligence, see L. Britt Snider, *The Agency and the Hill: CIA's Relationship with Congress, 1946–2004* (Washington, DC: Center for the Study of Intelligence, 2008), pp. 89–91. For more on polarization trends generally in elites and masses, see Pietro Nivola and David W. Brady, eds., *Red and Blue Nation?* Volumes 1 and 2 (Stanford, CA: and Washington, DC: Hoover Institution and Brookings Institution Press, 2006).

expertise in intelligence; and committee jurisdictions and policies that have fragmented Congress's *budgetary power* over executive branch intelligence agencies. These two weaknesses did not arise by accident; they were self-inflicted. In both areas, electoral incentives and internal congressional turf battles have led Congress to limit its own oversight capabilities even when the problems are well-known and the national security stakes are high. Ten years after 9/11, the United States has an intelligence oversight system that is well-designed to serve the re-election interests of individual legislators and protect congressional committee prerogatives, but poorly designed to serve the national interest.

OUTLINE OF THE BOOK

I begin in chapter 2 by asking what good oversight looks like. This question is more important and knottier than it seems. Political scientists and policymakers have never had a consensus working definition of "oversight" or what constitutes "effectiveness." But a review of the history of intelligence oversight; interviews with intelligence officials, legislators, and congressional staff; and quantitative oversight metrics all suggest that something is amiss. However one defines good oversight, Congress has not been doing it in intelligence for a very long time.

Chapter 3 examines existing research in both political science and intelligence studies and finds that both literatures have insights and limitations when it comes to understanding enduring intelligence oversight weaknesses. Political scientists seek generalities that obscure key realities of intelligence. Scholars in intelligence studies, on the other hand, emphasize the distinctive features of espionage and overlook the root causes of oversight dysfunction. The result is that one literature is too broad, the other too narrow. Taken together, however, they provide essential elements for understanding why intelligence oversight has remained so problematic for so long.

Chapter 4 turns from logic to data, comparing oversight activities of intelligence to other policy areas. Surprisingly, this kind of comparative analysis has never been done before. By applying the two most widely known oversight models (police patrol and fire alarm) to a range of policy issues and developing several original oversight data sets, Julie Quinn and I find that Congress is not overseeing nearly as much in intelligence as other policy domains. Electoral incentives explain why. Ironically, the same motives that foster responsiveness in some policy areas lead to neglect in others. The desire to win re-election naturally leads legislators to consider voter preferences, heed interest group demands, and cater to district industries and constituencies. But these considerations also encourage the average re-election minded representative to spend as little time as possible on intelligence issues. Why? Because intelligence is the worst of all worlds: a complicated policy area that requires large up-front investments of time to master but promises low political payoffs and a non-trivial degree of political risk. In short, intelligence oversight is always an uphill battle because the issue is always a political loser.

Chapter 5 moves the analytic lens from comparing oversight across policy committees to examining more closely what's wrong with intelligence oversight. I find two crucial institutional deficiencies: limited expertise and weak, fragmented budgetary authority. These are serious weaknesses. In politics, knowledge and money are two of the most potent weapons. As the old saying goes, information is power. And as Lee Hamilton once said, Washington lives by the golden rule: he who controls the gold makes the rules.[20] The intelligence committees lack both. Here, too, rational self-interest explains why.

Chapter 6 concludes by suggesting policy implications for the future of intelligence oversight. The picture is not encouraging. If

20. Lee Hamilton, testimony before SSCI, Hearing on Congressional Oversight, 110th Cong., 1st session, 13 November 2007.

my analysis is correct, then the sources of oversight dysfunction lie with electoral incentives and institutional prerogatives. These are not about to disappear any time soon. As David Mayhew argued thirty years ago, congressional rules and structures are designed in ways that maximize the re-election interests of individual members.[21] Intelligence after 9/11 is no exception. Congress's irrational oversight system has rational roots: Electoral incentives on the outside and the zero-sum nature of committee power on the inside provide powerful reasons for Congress to continue hobbling its own oversight capabilities even in today's post-9/11 national security environment.

21. David Mayhew, *The Electoral Connection* (New Haven: Yale University Press, 1974).

CHAPTER TWO

What Does Good Oversight Look Like, Anyway?

Congressional oversight of the executive branch has long been considered vital to American constitutional government. Never explicitly mentioned in the Constitution, Congress's oversight powers were instead implied and rooted in the principle of separation of powers. At the Constitutional Convention, the framers fought vigorously over many issues, but the necessity of establishing a system of separated powers with checks and balances was not one of them.[1] The founders agreed on the overriding importance of preventing despotism and the overriding value of dividing power to achieve that goal. Madison called separation of powers "the sacred maxim of free government."[2] *Federalist 51* famously noted, "If men were angels, no government would be necessary. If angels were to govern men, neither external nor internal controls on government would be necessary."[3]

---

1. James L. Sundquist, "The Constitutional Dilemma," in *Constitutional Reform and Effective Government* (Washington, DC: Brookings, 1992), pp. 1–21.
2. James Madison, *Federalist #47*, 1 February 1788. Accessed at Yale Law School Library Avalon project, http://avalon.law.yale.edu/18th_century/fed47.asp (4 May 2010).
3. *Federalist #51*, 8 February 1788. Accessed at Yale Law School Library Avalon project, http://avalon.law.yale.edu/18th_century/fed47.asp (4 May 2010).

Oversight was considered a core part of Congress's constitutional duties from the republic's earliest days. As Louis Fisher notes, "the framers understood that legislatures must oversee the executive branch."[4] Historian Arthur Schlesinger writes that the framers felt they did not need to delineate oversight powers in the Constitution because, "The power to make laws implied the power to see whether they were faithfully executed."[5] This implied power rested on two major foundations. First, Congress could not possibly fulfill its constitutional functions—including enacting laws, raising and supporting armies, impeaching and trying U.S. officials—without knowing what the executive branch was doing and assessing whether these activities satisfied statutory intent. Second, the Constitution's "necessary and proper clause"[6] gave Congress wide latitude to impose oversight responsibilities on the executive branch.[7]

At the Constitutional Convention, George Mason emphasized that members of Congress "are not only Legislators but they also possess inquisitorial powers. They must meet frequently to inspect the Conduct of the public offices."[8] Although oversight did not receive much more discussion at the Constitutional Convention, the American colonial legislatures and British Parliament

---

4. Louis Fisher, "Congressional Investigations: Subpoenas and Contempt Power," *Congressional Research Service Report* RL 31836, 2 April 2003, p. 1.

5. Arthur M. Schlesinger, Jr. and Roger Bruns, eds., *Congress Investigates: A Documented History, 1792–1974*, Vol. 1 (New York: Chelsea House, 1975), p. xix.

6. That clause states: "Congress shall have the power . . . To make all laws which shall be necessary and proper for carrying into Execution the foregoing Powers, and all other Powers vested by this Constitution in the Government of the United States, or in any Department or Officer thereof." U.S. Constitution, Article I, Sec. 8.

7. U.S. House Committee on House Administration, House Document No. 103–324, *History of the House of Representatives, 1789–1994* [hereafter *House History*], 103d Congress, 2d sess. (Washington, DC: GPO, 1994), p. 237.

8. *The Records of the Federal Convention of 1787*, at 206 (Farrand ed. 1937), cited in Fisher 2003, p. 1.

had long deemed the power to gather information part and parcel of their power to legislate.[9] Early actions of the fledging United States government suggest that these views of oversight were widely shared among the founders.[10] The First Congress of the United States acted quickly to impose reporting obligations on the executive. The 1789 Treasury Department Act required the Secretary of the Treasury "to make report, and give information to either branch of the legislature, in person or in writing (as he may be required), respecting all matters referred to him by the Senate or House of Representatives. . . ." The act also required the treasurer to report "on the third day of every session of Congress" copies of "all accounts by him . . . and a true and perfect account of the state of the treasury."[11] In 1792, by a vote of 44–10, Congress conducted its first executive branch investigation, examining a disastrous military campaign against frontier Indians led by General Arthur St. Clair. Congress's special investigative committee demanded executive branch documents and access to officials. President Washington complied, setting an important precedent that the legislature was entitled to receive executive branch information even in matters of national security.[12] This

9. Arthur M. Schlesinger, Jr., "Introduction," in Arthur M. Schlesinger, Jr. and Roger Bruns, eds., *Congress Investigates: A Documented History* (New York: Chelsea House, 1975) volume I, p. xix.

10. The House's own history notes, "A review of the primary documents — including James Madison's notes of the Convention debates, along with secondary sources—reveals only a few relevant references to Congress' power to review, monitor, or supervise the executive." U.S. House Committee on House Administration, House Document No. 103–324, *History of the House of Representatives, 1789–1994*, 103d Congress, 2d sess. (Washington, DC: GPO, 1994), p. 236, fn 10. For more, see *The Debates in the Federal Convention of 1787 Which Framed the Constitution of the United States of America* (reported by James Madison) (Westport, CT: Greenwood Press, 1920); Schlesinger and Bruns, 1975.

11. 1 Stat. 66 (1789). Accessed at http://www.ustreas.gov/education/fact-sheets/history/act-congress.shtml (28 June 2010).

12. Although Washington concurred that the House had a legitimate right to the documents, the president insisted on controlling the release of some of the papers, which set an equally important precedent of executive privilege. For more,

precedent was quickly followed. According to Leonard White's history, between 1815 and 1825 "the power to investigate became well fixed as an important means by which Congress discharged its duty of supervising the conduct of the administration."[13] Congress's more regularized reporting requirements also grew. In 1822, there were so many reports being submitted to Congress from executive branch agencies and officials that the House adopted a rule requiring the clerk to provide each member with "a list of the reports which it is the duty of any officer or Department to make to Congress . . . ."[14] By 1885, political scientist and future president Woodrow Wilson asserted in an influential book that Congress's oversight function was just as important as its lawmaking role.[15] Noted Wilson, "It is the proper duty of a representative body to look diligently into every affair of government and to talk much about what it sees. It is meant to be the eyes and the voice, and to embody the wisdom and will of its constituents." Congress's "informing function," Wilson concluded, "should be preferred even to its legislative function."[16]

Yet, defining exactly what oversight means and what effective oversight looks like, particularly with the rise of the modern administrative state, is not quite so easy. Three reasons explain why. First, "good" oversight lies in the eyes of the beholder. What

---

see Fisher 2003, pp. 2–4; U.S. House Committee on House Administration, House Document No. 103–324, *History of the House of Representatives, 1789–1994*, 103d Congress, 2d sess. (Washington, DC: GPO, 1994), p. 241.

13. Leonard D. White, *The Jeffersonians: A Study in Administrative History, 1801–1829* (New York: Macmillan Company, 1951), p. 100. For more, see U.S. House Committee on House Administration, House Document No. 103–324, *History of the House of Representatives, 1789–1994*, 103d Congress, 2d sess. (Washington, DC: GPO, 1994), pp. 233–66.

14. House Rule III, cl. 2, 1822, cited in *House History*, p. 246, fn 45.

15. Woodrow Wilson, *Congressional Government* (Boston: Houghton Mifflin, 1885).

16. Woodrow Wilson, *Congressional Government*, 6th edition (Cleveland, Ohio: The World Publishing Company, 1961), p. 198.

constitutes optimal offshore oil drilling regulation is different for the Sierra Club than British Petroleum. Oversight does not take place in a political vacuum where legislators conduct a Spock-like assessment of options, costs, and benefits. Instead, oversight is embedded in politics and intertwined with policy advocacy on behalf of constituents, groups, and their interests.[17]

Second, as James Q. Wilson has noted, government agencies often have conflicting mandates.[18] Such contradictory missions ensure that "good oversight" is much more nuanced and tricky than it first appears, involving tradeoffs across missions and contending stakeholders who have vested interests in different things. The Forest Service, for example, was originally designed to facilitate timber mining in public lands, but now also has responsibility for preserving those lands for public recreation and wildlife conservation. The Department of Homeland Security is charged both with letting people into the United States and keeping terrorists out. Navigating among these conflicting interests, agencies, and their congressional overseers can never please everyone. Although intelligence agencies have a more unified mission—providing information that gives policymakers decision advantage to protect American lives and interests—intelligence agencies are not immune to this problem. The Detainee Treatment Act of 2005, for example, which sought to circumscribe interrogation methods for detainees in defense department custody, is viewed as robust and necessary oversight by some and irresponsible congressional micromanagement by others.

The third reason why good oversight is hard to define is that many important oversight activities are simply invisible or impossible to gauge. Telephone calls, e-mails, and other informal staff

17. Ogul 1976; Joel Aberbach, "Improving Oversight: The Endless Task of Congress," *Society* 40 (Nov/Dec 2002), pp. 60–63.
18. James Q. Wilson, *Bureaucracy: What Government Agencies Do and Why They Do It* (New York: Basic Books, 1989).

oversight activities happen all the time, but cannot be counted in data sets or measured in other systematic ways. Even more important, the very *possibility* that an agency's action might trigger a future congressional hearing (what some intelligence officials refer to as "the threat of the green felt table"), or some other sort of congressional response, can influence executive branch decisions from the outset. This kind of anticipatory oversight can be powerful, but from the outside it looks like no oversight at all.[19]

Despite these inherent definitional limitations, weak intelligence oversight is a reasonable and useful point of departure. Effective oversight may be hard to define, but ineffectual oversight is often easy to see. The historical record, interviews with legislators and intelligence officials, and quantitative evidence all suggest that Congress has struggled with its intelligence oversight duties for decades.

HISTORY

1947–1970s: Congressional "Undersight".[20]   From the CIA's creation in 1947 until the mid-1970s, Congress's oversight "system" was not much of a system at all. Intelligence oversight was fleeting, ad hoc, and sporadic.[21] Rather than creating a new oversight committee explicitly dedicated to intelligence matters, oversight was divvied up between sub-panels of the powerful Appropriations and Armed Services Committees, which had little

19. Barry Weingast and Mark Moran, "Bureaucratic Discretion or Congressional Control? Regulatory Policymaking by the Federal Trade Commission," *Journal of Political Economy* 91 (October 1983), pp. 775–800.

20. Barry M. Blechman, *The Politics of National Security: Congress and U.S. Defense Policy* (New York: Oxford University Press, 1990).

21. For an alternative view, see David M. Barrett, *The CIA and Congress: The Untold Story from Truman to Kennedy* (Lawrence: University Press of Kansas, 2005).

time for or interest in intelligence activities. A handful of committee leaders, including the chairmen, met to discuss intelligence issues only about two or three times a year, always in secret, and informally.[22] In 1951, the CIA subcommittee of the Senate Armed Services Committee met just once.[23] The Senate Appropriations Committee's CIA panel met once in 1956 and not at all in 1957.[24] More sensitive matters were handled through one-on-one sessions between the CIA director and the individual committee chairman. But these, too, were infrequent and informal. "It is not a question of reluctance on the part of the CIA officials to speak to us," said Senator Leverett Saltonstall (R-MA), who served on both the Senate Appropriations and Armed Services Committees during the 1950s. "Instead it is a question of our reluctance, if you will, to seek information and knowledge on subjects which I personally, as a Member of Congress and as a citizen, would rather not have."[25] Indeed, CIA officials struggled to get more congressional attention. "There were very loose reins on us at the time," recalled CIA legislative counsel Walter Pforzheimer, "because the Congress believed in what we were doing. It wasn't that we were attempting to hide anything. Our main problem was, we couldn't get them to sit still and listen."[26]

It is important to underscore that this loose system arose by choice, not chance. In 1946, just as Congress was debating the creation of the Central Intelligence Agency, it passed the Legislative Reorganization Act, which directed congressional standing committees to "exercise continuous watchfulness" over the agencies and

22. For more, see Frank J. Smist, Jr., *Congress Oversees the United States Intelligence Community, 1947–1994*, 2nd ed (Knoxville: University of Tennessee Press, 1994); Snider 2008.

23. CIA draft study, Vol. 1, 38, cited in Snider 2008, p. 8.

24. Snider 2008, p. 18.

25. *Congressional Record*, 1956, p. 5924.

26. Britt Snider interview of Pforzheimer, 11 January 1988, p. 16, printed in Snider 2008, pp. 9–10.

programs in their jurisdiction. The landmark oversight act also dramatically improved congressional staff capabilities and resources to make oversight more vigorous.[27] Yet at precisely the moment legislators were thinking up ways to bolster oversight in other areas, they chose not to create an oversight committee for the new CIA. Over the next thirty years, legislative majorities voted repeatedly and overwhelmingly against more than two hundred bills to consolidate and improve their intelligence oversight system.[28]

Congress later gave itself low marks for oversight during this period. The Church Committee concluded in its 1976 report that "The legislative branch ha[d] been remiss in exercising its control over the intelligence agencies"[29] for nearly three decades. Notably, Congress's lackluster intelligence oversight from the 1940s to the 1970s remained remarkably resilient and consistent despite changes in party control of the House and Senate, despite fourteen years of unified government and sixteen years of divided government, and despite nearly an even split between Democratic and Republican presidents.

1970s–Present: Routinization. The 1970s brought a confluence of events that gave rise to a new and improved, more formal oversight system. The Vietnam War and the Watergate scandal bred a profound distrust of government and an unprecedented period of congressional activism. Gone were the days when legislators automatically deferred to the executive branch. In addition, there was deep suspicion about the CIA's role in the Watergate

27. Public Law 601, 79th Congress, 2d sess. 2 August 1946.

28. Amy B. Zegart, *Flawed by Design: The Evolution of the CIA, JCS, and NSC* (Stanford, CA: Stanford University Press, 1999), p. 193; Harry Howe Ransom, "Congress and the Intelligence Agencies," *Proceedings of the Academy of Political Science* Vol. 32, No. 1 (1975), p. 162.

29. U.S. Senate, Select Committee to Study Governmental Operations with Respect to Intelligence Activities of the United States (Church Committee), *Final Report*, 94th Cong., 2d sess. [April 26, 1976], S. Rept. 94–755, Serial 13133-3-8, p. 11.

break-in (all five men arrested bugging the Democratic National Committee headquarters had ties to the agency) and President Nixon's use of the agency in the subsequent cover-up (we now know that the White House asked the CIA to interfere with the FBI's Watergate investigation but CIA Director Richard Helms refused).[30] Against this backdrop came press reports in September 1974 revealing that the CIA was undertaking a covert operation to destabilize Salvador Allende's democratically elected Marxist regime in Chile. Just three months later, the *New York Times* ran a page one story detailing how the CIA had been engaging in a "massive illegal domestic intelligence operation" against anti-war protesters and other dissidents in the United States, in direct violation of the agency's statutory charter.[31]

With all of these scandals swirling, the Senate launched an investigation led by Senator Frank Church (D-Idaho).[32] Lasting fifteen months, holding 126 formal hearings, conducting more than 800 interviews, and releasing 14 volumes of hearings and reports, the Church Committee was the first serious examination of CIA activities and one of the most sweeping congressional investigations in U.S. history. The Committee found widespread abuses in the CIA and FBI, including assassination plots against foreign leaders, domestic spying on Americans, domestic covert action, and drug experimentation on unwitting subjects. The Committee's final report did not mince words: the Intelligence Community required major and immediate changes to bring covert activities under congressional and constitutional control.

30. Snider 2008, p. 29.
31. Seymour Hersh, "Huge CIA Operation Reported in U.S. Against Antiwar Forces, Other Dissidents in Nixon Years," *New York Times*, 22 December 1974.
32. The House also launched an investigation led by Congressman Lucien Nedzi (D-MI) and then Otis Pike (D-NY), but that effort was riddled with leaks and political infighting and never received the same kind of attention and imprimatur that the Church Committee did.

Many changes did result. Most important, the House and Senate soon created permanent select committees on intelligence to oversee the CIA and the rest of the Intelligence Community. These committees routinized intelligence oversight for the first time. The days of ad hoc and informal relations between agencies and Congress were over. With the new committees came new standard reporting requirements, new expectations, and more legal obligations.

In addition, the Senate, and to a lesser extent the House, took steps to mitigate partisanship on the new intelligence committees. Both chambers decided to make the intelligence committees select rather than standing committees, which meant that members were personally selected by party leaders in each chamber, not the party caucuses.[33] The Senate Select Committee on Intelligence was designed to have fifteen members, only eight of whom could come from the majority party, thus ensuring a nearly even party split no matter how large the proportion of the majority party in the full Senate. Instead of a ranking member, the SSCI had a vice chairman chosen from the minority party who would preside in the absence of the chairman. This was a substantial departure from the customary practice of having the next most senior majority party member serve in the chair's absence. The House Permanent Select Committee on Intelligence (HPSCI) did not adopt the Senate's bipartisan composition or minority party vice chairman. But House Speaker Thomas P. "Tip" O'Neill (D-MA) made clear at the time that the new intelligence committee would "deliberate and act in a nonpartisan manner."[34] Data show that the House and Senate Intelligence Committees generally have not been filled with party outliers on either the left or

---

33. Senate committee chairmen and ranking members, however, continued to be chosen by party caucuses. See Snider 2008, p. 51.
34. Quote from Smist 1994, p. 216.

right. Instead, they have typically been filled with legislators who are more moderate than their party colleagues.

Figures 2.1 and 2.2 compare the partisanship of Democrats and Republicans serving on the House Intelligence Committee to their House party colleagues overall from 1989 to 2006. Polarization is measured by comparing the median scores legislators received from Americans for Democratic Action (ADA). ADA scores are the most widely used measures of party ideology and run from zero to one hundred, where zero is the most conservative and one hundred is the most liberal. To improve the accuracy of comparisons across time, I adjusted ADA scores using Groseclose, Levitt, and Snyder's algorithm.[35] Figure 2.1 examines Democrats, comparing the median ADA score for Democrats serving on the House Intelligence Committee to the median ADA score for House Democrats overall. As the figure shows, Intelligence Committee Democrats scored either the same or lower than their House colleagues for fourteen of the eighteen years examined. This means that the median Intelligence Committee Democrat was *the same or more conservative* than the median House Democrat. Only in 1989, 1990, 1991, and 2006 were House Intelligence Committee Democrats skewing more liberal than House Democrats overall. ADA scores of House Republicans reveal a similar centrist trend. Figure 2.2 shows that in fourteen of the eighteen years, the median House Intelligence Committee Republican was the *same or more liberal* than the median House Republican overall. Figures 2.3 and 2.4 show the same analysis for the Senate. Here, too, we find that in fifteen out of eighteen years, both Republican and Democratic Intelligence Committee medians were either the same or more moderate

---

35. Tim Groseclose, Steven D. Levitt, and James M. Snyder, Jr., "Comparing Interest Group Scores across Time and Chambers: adjusted ADA Scores for the U.S. Congress," *American Political Science Review* 93, No. 1 (1999), pp. 33–50.

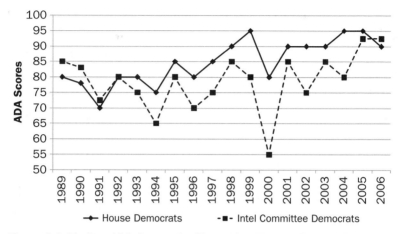

Figure 2.1 Median ADA Scores for House Intelligence Committee Democrats vs. House Democrats Overall, 1989–2006

Sources: For raw ADA scores, see Americans for Democratic Action, available at http://www.adaction.org/pages/publications/voting-records.php. Scores were adjusted with the Groseclose, Levitt, and Snyder algorithm to make them comparable across years. Tim Groseclose, Steven D. Levitt, and James M. Snyder, Jr., "Comparing Interest Group Scores across Time and Chambers: Adjusted ADA Scores for the U.S. Congress," *American Political Science Review* 93, 1 (1999), pp. 33–50. Annual membership of the Senate Select Committee on Intelligence and the House Permanent Select Committee on Intelligence from *Congressional Directory*.

than their respective Senate party medians overall. Senate Intelligence Committee Democratic medians were higher (more liberal) than the Senate overall only in 1999, 2003, and 2004. Intelligence Committee Republican median scores were lower (more conservative) than the chamber Republican median only in 2001, 2002, and 2005. In sum, while both parties have grown more partisan and polarized over time, these data suggest that Democrats and Republicans have not appointed legislators from the extreme ends of their party to the intelligence committees.

In short, the creation of permanent House and Senate Select Committees on Intelligence in 1976–77 established for the first time a serious focus on intelligence agencies and programs by committees whose members were supposed to act in a more bipar-

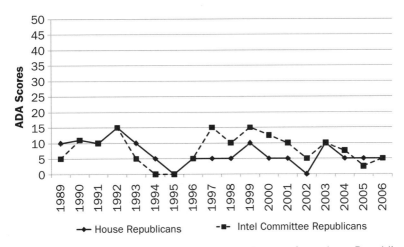

Figure 2.2 Median ADA Scores for House Intelligence Committee Republicans vs. House Republicans Overall, 1989–2006

Sources: For raw ADA scores, see Americans for Democratic Action, available at http://www.adaction.org/pages/publications/voting-records.php. Scores were adjusted with the Groseclose, Levitt, and Snyder algorithm to make them comparable across years. Tim Groseclose, Steven D. Levitt, and James M. Snyder, Jr., "Comparing Interest Group Scores across Time and Chambers: Adjusted ADA Scores for the U.S. Congress," *American Political Science Review* 93, 1 (1999), pp. 33–50. Annual membership of the Senate Select Committee on Intelligence and the House Permanent Select Committee on Intelligence from *Congressional Directory.*

tisan fashion. These changes were, and still are, viewed as a major departure and improvement from earlier arrangements.

Yet, serious oversight weaknesses remained. Indeed, the Church Committee ultimately failed to obtain many of the oversight reforms it sought. Church and his colleagues made three principal recommendations: (1) that Congress pass new legislation spelling out each agency's charter as well as its relationship with Congress; (2) that Congress pass a statutory ban on many covert activities such as political assassinations; and (3) that Congress establish much stronger oversight mechanisms, including a new permanent intelligence committee whose prior approval would be required for all covert activities. It took sixteen years to get intelligence charter legislation. By the time it passed, the Cold War had ended,

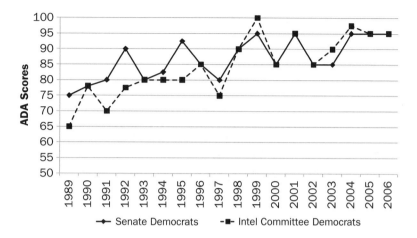

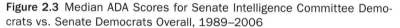

Figure 2.3 Median ADA Scores for Senate Intelligence Committee Democrats vs. Senate Democrats Overall, 1989–2006

Sources: For raw ADA scores, see Americans for Democratic Action, available at http://www.adaction.org/pages/publications/voting-records.php. Scores were adjusted with the Groseclose, Levitt, and Snyder algorithm to make them comparable across years. Tim Groseclose, Steven D. Levitt, and James M. Snyder, Jr., "Comparing Interest Group Scores across Time and Chambers: Adjusted ADA Scores for the U.S. Congress," *American Political Science Review* 93, 1 (1999), pp. 33–50. Annual membership of the Senate Select Committee on Intelligence and the House Permanent Select Committee on Intelligence from *Congressional Directory*.

and the functions of intelligence agencies were in flux. Congress never succeeded in banning assassinations by statute; instead, assassinations are prohibited by executive order, which any president can change with the stroke of a pen. And Congress never gained the right to legally approve or reject covert operations. Subsequent laws required only that the intelligence oversight committees *be informed* of covert activities by the executive branch. Equally important, as I discuss more fully in chapter 5, Congress ensured that the new permanent select oversight committees would emerge with two serious institutional deficiencies: term limits for the legislators serving on them that prevented the development of intelligence policy expertise; and budgetary authority fragmented between the intelligence committees and

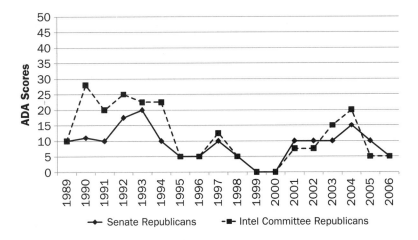

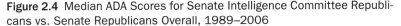

Figure 2.4 Median ADA Scores for Senate Intelligence Committee Republicans vs. Senate Republicans Overall, 1989–2006

Sources: For raw ADA scores, see Americans for Democratic Action, available at http://www.adaction.org/pages/publications/voting-records.php. Scores were adjusted with the Groseclose, Levitt, and Snyder algorithm to make them comparable across years. Tim Groseclose, Steven D. Levitt, and James M. Snyder, Jr., "Comparing Interest Group Scores across Time and Chambers: Adjusted ADA Scores for the U.S. Congress," *American Political Science Review* 93, 1 (1999), pp. 33–50. Annual membership of the Senate Select Committee on Intelligence and the House Permanent Select Committee on Intelligence from *Congressional Directory*.

the appropriations committees, which ensured that Congress would have weak budgetary power over executive branch intelligence agencies. These and other weaknesses have plagued the intelligence committees ever since.

Congress's oversight problems were hardly secret. From 1991 to 2001, a dozen major unclassified reports examined critical challenges in intelligence and counterterrorism.[36] Seven of them

36. The dozen studies included six blue-ribbon, bipartisan presidential commissions. These were: Commission on the Roles and Capabilities of the United States Intelligence Community (Aspin-Brown Commission), *Preparing for the 21st Century: An Appraisal of U.S. Intelligence*, (Washington, DC: Government Printing Office, 1996); Commission to Assess the Organization of the Federal Government to Combat the Proliferation of Weapons of Mass Destruction (Deutch Commission), *Combating Proliferation of Weapons of Mass Destruction* (Washington,

concluded that congressional oversight urgently needed fixing. Together the reports issued nineteen recommendations for reform.[37] Congress did not implement a single one. In fact, of all the organizations in the U.S. intelligence system, the only one with a zero reform implementation record in the 1990s wasn't the FBI or the National Security Agency or the CIA. It was Congress.

DC: U.S. GPO, 1999); Advisory Panel to Assess Domestic Response Capabilities for Terrorism Involving Weapons of Mass Destruction (Gilmore Commission), *First Annual Report to the President and the Congress: Assessing the Threat* (Washington, DC: U.S. GPO, 1999) and *Second Annual Report of the President and the Congress: Toward a National Strategy for Combating Terrorism* (Washington, DC: U.S. GPO, 2000); National Commission on Terrorism (Bremer Commission), *Countering the Changing Threat of International Terrorism* (Washington, DC: U.S. GPO, 2000); U.S. Commission on National Security/21st Century (Hart-Rudman Commission), *Road Map For National Security: Imperative for Change*, Phase III Report, http://www.au.af.mil./au/awc/awcgate/nssg/phaseIIIfr.pdf, 15 February 2001; and Commission on the Advancement of Federal Law Enforcement (Webster Commission), *Law Enforcement in a New Century and a Changing World: Improving the Administration of Federal Law Enforcement* (Washington, DC: U.S. GPO, 2000). Three reports came from government reviews. These were: National Performance Review, "The Intelligence Community: Recommendations and Actions," in *From Red Tape to Results: Creating a Government that Works Better and Costs Less* (Washington, DC: U.S. GPO, September 1993) and National Performance Review, *National Performance Review Phase II Initiatives: An Intelligence Community Report* (Washington, DC: U.S. GPO, 1995); House Permanent Select Committee on Intelligence, *IC21: The Intelligence Community in the 21st Century* (Washington, DC: U.S. GPO, 1996); and Federal Bureau of Investigation, *Draft FBI Strategic Plan: 1998–2003, Keeping Tomorrow Safe* (Washington, DC: U.S. GPO, 1998). Three reports came from nonpartisan think tanks. These were: Council on Foreign Relations Independent Task Force, *Making Intelligence Smarter: The Future of U.S. Intelligence* (New York: The Council on Foreign Relations, 1996); Twentieth Century Fund Task Force on the Future of U.S. Intelligence, *In from the Cold: The Report of the Twentieth Century Fund Task Force on the Future of U.S. Intelligence* (New York: Twentieth Century Fund Press, 1996); and National Institute for Public Policy, *Modernizing Intelligence: Structure and Change for the 21st Century* (Fairfax, VA: National Institute for Public Policy, 2002). For more about these studies' recommendations, see Zegart 2007, pp. 15–42.

37. These were the Aspin-Brown commission, the Bremer commission, Council on Foreign Relations task force, Deutch commission, Gilmore commission, Hart-Rudman commission, and House Intelligence Staff Study, *IC21*.

INTERVIEWS

Personal interviews complement the historical overview presented above, enabling us to get inside the minds of those who have had to consider what oversight means and live with the realities of oversight both inside Congress and in the intelligence agencies oversight is designed to monitor. Over the past several years, I have interviewed more than eighty current and former intelligence officials, legislators, and Capitol Hill staffers, many of them repeatedly. These interviews reveal a widely shared view that intelligence oversight ideally fulfills four roles:

(1) **Policeman:** Ensuring that intelligence policies and activities fall within the bounds of the law
(2) **Board of Directors:** Setting strategic guidance and ensuring that resources are matched against priorities
(3) **Coach:** Continuously examining and improving current programs and practices
(4) **Ambassador:** Generating public trust and support for the vital functions that secret intelligence agencies play in U.S. national security.[38]

Although individual participants in the intelligence system emphasized some roles more than others—with legislators and their staffs focusing more on legal compliance and intelligence officials highlighting Congress's public support function—nearly all of them complained that oversight was nowhere close to meeting their expectations. And most believed that oversight was consistently ineffective and getting more so. In the spring of 2009, then CIA Director and former Congressman Leon Panetta said, "I do

---

38. See also Fisher 2003; Walter Olesezek, "Congressional Oversight: An Overview," *Congressional Research Service Report* R41079, 22 February 2010.

believe in the responsibility of the Congress not only to oversee our operations but to share in the responsibility of making sure that we have the resources and capability to help protect this country. The only way that's going to work is if both parties are working in the same direction." And yet, Panetta added, "There's been a lot of poison in the well in these last few years."[39] Another senior intelligence official noted that oversight had deteriorated so much during his career, "I don't even know what good oversight looks like anymore."[40] Overseers agreed. One legislator who served on a congressional intelligence committee called oversight "horrible,"[41] and noted that "In the last six years, we have not done our job to be an independent branch of government." When asked what it would take to improve the intelligence budget process, he laughed and said, "Oh God. Somebody in Congress would have to die."[42]

OVERSIGHT METRICS

These impressions are supported by the two metrics most frequently used to measure oversight: hearing and legislative productivity. Although not all oversight is good oversight, it stands to reason that more hearings and bills usually suggest a more engaged legislature.

Tracking hearings held by fifteen House and Senate committees in 1985, 1990, 1995, 2000, and 2005, I found that the intelligence committees ranked at the bottom every year except one.[43]

39. Interview by author, 18 May 2009.
40. Interview by author, 19 August 2009.
41. Interview by author, 14 March 2009.
42. Interview by author, 19 October 2006.
43. Senate committees examined were: Foreign Relations; Science, Commerce and Transportation; Finance; Homeland Security and Governmental Affairs; Health, Education, Labor, and Pensions; Environment and Public Works; and Intelligence. House committees examined were Foreign Relations; Energy and

The difference in activity levels is striking. In 2005, the House Intelligence Committee held just 23 hearings (including both classified and unclassified hearings), compared to 77 in the Energy and Commerce Committee, 91 in the Oversight and Government Reform Committee, and 104 hearings held by the Foreign Affairs Committee. Intelligence committees also trailed behind others in producing legislation.[44] In a comparison of legislative productivity among four major Senate policy committees, Intelligence again ranked last. Between 1985 and 2005, the Senate Intelligence Committee considered an average of just six bills per year. By contrast, the Senate Foreign Relations Committee considered an average of 118 bills per year, the Senate Banking Committee considered 161 bills, and the Senate Commerce Committee considered an average of 241 bills each year. It is important to note that some committees, particularly those that deal with regulatory issues, are likely to produce and consider far more bills each year than Intelligence. However, this means that the intelligence committees should have comparatively more time to devote to other oversight activities (such as hearings), which has not been the case. In short, these traditional activity measures show that even with the emergence of the intelligence committees, Congress spends more time overseeing other policy domains than intelligence.[45]

To be sure, history, interviews, and congressional activity data

---

Commerce; Science and Technology; Ways and Means; Oversight and Government Reform; Education and Labor; Transportation and Infrastructure; and Intelligence. These committees were chosen to replicate and extend Aberbach's empirical analysis of oversight activities between the 1960s and 1980s. Hearing data from U.S. Congress, *Congressional Record Daily Digest*, 99th–109th Cong., accessed via LexisNexis Congressional.

44. Johnson finds that from 1975 to 1990, the Congressional intelligence committees averaged fewer than two public hearings a year. Loch K. Johnson, *U.S. Intelligence in a Hostile World* (New Haven: Yale University Press, 1996), p. 96.

45. Zegart and Quinn 2010.

can never paint a complete picture of oversight efforts, their quality, or impact. There is always more to the story, particularly in the world of classified information. The picture they do paint, however, is informative, suggesting that at the very least, effective oversight is a dubious proposition.

SUMMARY

While good oversight is difficult to define and measure, it is fair to say that intelligence oversight has struggled for a long time. The history of intelligence oversight is not encouraging. Personal interviews suggest that almost nobody in the intelligence business thinks oversight is working well, even after the creation of the permanent intelligence oversight committees. And the best objective indicators show that Congress is expending substantially less effort holding hearings and considering bills in intelligence than in other policy areas. Problematic oversight, in short, is a reasonable point of departure. The question is not so much whether intelligence oversight is weak, but why.

CHAPTER THREE

Goldilocks and the Intelligence Oversight Literature

For decades, scholars have hotly debated why congressional oversight often looks so ineffective.[1] Yet our understanding of *intelligence* oversight remains surprisingly underdeveloped. This is primarily because intelligence oversight lies at the crossroads of two academic fields: political science and intelligence studies. As I discuss more below, each field contributes essential insights but neither captures the full picture. The political science literature is conceptually strong but empirically weak when it comes to explaining the intelligence world. Work in intelligence studies has the opposite problem, offering rich, detailed histories of intelligence oversight but little analytic traction to understand broader oversight dynamics over time or the underlying forces that cause them. In short, one literature pays too little attention to intelligence, the other pays too much attention to intelligence. Achieving the Goldilocks "just right" mix between abstract theory and political reality has proven to be difficult and elusive.

---

1. Weingast and Moran 1983; Mathew D. McCubbins and Thomas Schwartz, "Congressional Oversight Overlooked: Police Patrol versus Fire Alarm," *American Journal of Political Science* 28 (February 1984), pp. 165–179. But see Joel D. Aberbach, *Keeping a Watchful Eye: The Politics of Congressional Oversight* (Washington, DC: Brookings, 1990).

POLITICAL SCIENCE

In 1968, John F. Bibby noted that oversight was Congress's neglected function.[2] Since then, studies of congressional oversight have become a growth industry in political science, making careers and spawning countless books and academic journal articles. Three reasons explain this surging attention. First, political scientists are drawn to questions of power, and oversight is all about power—understanding when, how, and why legislators willingly delegate some of their own authority to unelected executive branch officials. Second, oversight involves Congress, and Congress does things that can be counted such as voting, passing bills, and holding hearings. Particularly compared to other political science topics (such as presidential decision-making or international relations), oversight is a data gold mine. And in the academic world, data is the name of the game, particularly data that can be subjected to quantitative analysis rather than "softer," harder-to-measure qualitative methods. Third and finally, political scientists have long favored importing methods and theories from economics, and oversight has proven well-suited to both.

This literature provides three important insights and possesses two serious limitations for understanding congressional intelligence oversight.

Insight #1: Incentives Drive Behavior. Political science approaches focus on what makes people alike, not what makes them different. Rational choice analysis, which is the discipline's dominant paradigm, contends that all individuals, whatever their personalities, idiosyncrasies, wants, and needs, act in predictable and

---

2. John F. Bibby, "Congress' Neglected Function," in *The Republican Papers*, ed. Melvin R. Laird (New York: Praeger, 1968).

systematic ways for predictable and systematic reasons. Namely, they select alternatives and conduct activities that they expect will maximize their benefits and minimize their costs. In politics, individuals are driven by the incentives of office to seek the highest net *political* advantages. There is no normative judgment here. Rational choice theory attempts to describe the way the political world works, not the way reformers wish it to be.[3]

For members of Congress, net political benefits boil down to one: winning re-election. As David Mayhew famously noted in 1974, electoral victory is usually not a legislator's only goal, but it is always their primary one, "the goal that must be achieved over and over if other ends are to be entertained."[4] This electoral connection is a powerful motivator. It explains why all legislators, regardless of party, district, or political era, behave in the ways they do.

Committee assignments in Congress illustrate the point. It should surprise no one that the Senate's Subcommittee on Oceans, Atmosphere, Fisheries, and Coast Guard is filled with members from coastal states while the Senate Agriculture Committee has an abundance of senators from places like Kansas, Iowa, and Nebraska. The reason is simple. Because legislators prefer winning re-election to losing, they seek committee assignments that can best deliver benefits to folks back home. The political calculations that drive oversight activities are less obvious but no

---

3. Amy Zegart, "Implementing Change: Organizational Challenges," in Baruch Fishhoff and Cherie Chauvin, eds., *Intelligence Analysis: Behavioral and Social Scientific Foundations* (Washington, DC: National Academies Press, 2011), p. 321. Three seminal works in rational choice are Kenneth J. Arrow, *Social Choice and Individual Values* (New York: Wiley, 1951); Anthony Downs, *An Economic Theory of Democracy* (New York: Harper and Row, 1957); and Mancur Olson, *The Logic of Collective Action* (Cambridge, MA: Harvard University Press, 1965). For an important critique, see Donald P. Green and Ian Shapiro, *Pathologies of Rational Choice Theory: A Critique of Applications in Political Science* (New Haven: Yale University Press, 1994).
4. Mayhew 1974, p. 16.

different. Electoral incentives mean that legislators will engage in greater oversight the more they are rewarded for it by constituents and organized interest groups, and the less costly oversight activities are to them—in terms of the time demanded, the activities forgone, the expertise required, and the staff resources needed. Understanding oversight dynamics starts by getting inside a legislator's cost-benefit mindset, asking whether the political advantages of any particular action are worth the political costs.

Insight #2: Individually Rational Decisions Can Produce Bad Collective Results. Political science research also cautions that individually rational decisions can produce bad collective outcomes. The classic example is the tragedy of the commons, where individual farmers seek to gain personal advantage by allowing their sheep to graze as much as possible on public lands. Yet, because every farmer makes the same cost-benefit calculation, they all make the same choice. Overgrazing ensues, the fields become infertile, and everyone suffers. Present-day tragedy-of-the-commons problems abound. Nobody likes wasteful government spending, but every member of Congress has strong incentives to draft legislative earmarks to fund his district's pet projects, leading to wasteful earmark proliferation. (More on that later.) When the stock market plummets, the reaction among investors is often to avoid bigger losses by selling fast. But when so many respond to these incentives in the same way, the market plunges even more. Rational behavior for one becomes detrimental for all. This same logic explains in part why intelligence agencies in the Pentagon and other parts of the U.S. Intelligence Community have historically fought against centralized control by the CIA director and his successor, the Director of National Intelligence, even though doing so hinders the coordination and collaboration essential to intelligence success. One reason agency employees circumvent or resist central directives is that they see personal or organizational benefits to protecting their own agency's turf and costs to ceding it.[5] The result, however, is that the entire intelligence system suffers.[6]

In the world of intelligence oversight, this insight suggests a paradox. Individual legislators can have very good electoral reasons to give intelligence oversight short shrift, but the result is often rules, norms, and practices that undermine Congress's oversight of the Intelligence Community, degrade Congress's institutional powers vis-à-vis the executive branch, and ultimately hinder the effective performance of U.S. intelligence agencies. Little things add up. What may be good for each legislator may be very bad for Congress, and the country, as a whole.

Insight #3: Congress Defers More (and Oversees Less) in Predictable Circumstances.   Third and finally, a great deal of work in political science finds that Congress delegates authority and defers to the executive branch more in some cases than others. These decisions are not made willy-nilly, but are based on interests, incentives, and history. The most obvious case is foreign policy, which has long been considered more of an executive branch affair warranting greater congressional deference than domestic policy matters.[7] In 1966, Aaron Wildavsky noted that the difference was

5. There are also pathological and psychological reasons for resisting centralization, including rigid adherence to outdated agency cultures, traditions, and identities; and aversion to change more generally.

6. Zegart 2011, p. 322.

7. As noted in chapter 1, expansive presidential authority is more rooted in the structure of government and history than in explicit provisions of the Constitution. The Constitution leaves much unclear and unsaid. The framers mention no general foreign policy authority, no power to recognize or break diplomatic relations, no power to declare policy doctrines or call an end to military hostilities. Moreover, the powers that are specified seem to fall somewhere between the executive and legislative branches. Though the Senate ratifies treaties, the president alone bears the responsibility for negotiating them. Similarly, the power to declare war is lodged with Congress but the president's powers as commander-in-chief suggest an executive responsibility and authority to direct U.S. military

so stark, it was as though there were two presidencies.[8] Others
have found that Congress delegates more authority to executive
branch agencies when issue complexity rises and public salience
of the issues at hand falls.[9] Conversely, when issue complexity is
low and issue salience is high, Congress should exert more control over the bureaucracy.

Just how complexity and salience play out in intelligence, however, is not so clear-cut. Intelligence scandals and controversies
may generate tremendous national press coverage and appear to
be highly salient. But the important thing is whether the intelligence issue is salient *to voters back home*. It usually is not. As I
note in chapter 4, even major foreign policy issues like the Cold
War's end or the Iraq War usually rank low on the list of voter
concerns in presidential elections and even lower in congressional
elections. Legislators know their particular constituents care far
more about matters closer to home. And because most of intelligence oversight is secret, the public usually will not know whether

defenses. Particularly since 9/11, scholars and policymakers have vigorously debated just where the appropriate bounds of executive authority should lie. As Edward Corwin noted half a century ago, the Constitution provides little more than
"an invitation to struggle for the privilege of directing American foreign policy."
Edward S. Corwin, *The President: Office and Powers*, 4th ed (New York: New York
University Press, 1957), p. 171.

8. Aaron Wildavsky, "The Two Presidencies," Trans-Action 4 (1966), pp. 7–14,
reprinted in Aaron Wildavsky, *The Beleaguered Presidency* (New Brunswick, NJ:
Transaction 1991), p. 29.

9. Evan Ringquist, Jeff Worsham, Marc Allen Eisner, "Salience, Complexity,
and the Legislative Direction of Regulatory Bureaucracies," *Journal of Public Administration Research and Theory*, Vol. 13, no. 2 (2003), pp. 141–64; Kathleen
Bawn, "Choosing Strategies to Control the Bureaucracy: Statutory Constraints,
Oversight, and the Committee System," *Journal of Law, Economics, and Organization* 131, no. 1 (1997), pp. 101–26; Kathleen Bawn, "Political Control versus Expertise: Congressional Choices about Administrative Procedures," *American Political
Science Review* 89, no. 1 (1995), pp. 62–73; William Gormley, "Regulatory Issue
Networks in a Federal System," *Polity* 18, no. 4 (1986), pp. 595–620; David Epstein and Sharyn O'Halloran, *Delegating Powers* (Cambridge University Press,
1999).

Congress takes action or not anyway. In short, the political science literature tells us that Congress will exercise less oversight in matters of national security than domestic policy, but it does not tell us much more than that.

These broad insights are coupled with substantial limitations. The most significant weakness of the political science literature is that none of the major work on oversight actually examines *intelligence* oversight. Instead, the vast majority of oversight research has focused on domestic regulatory agencies such as the Interstate Commerce Commission, Federal Trade Commission, and Environmental Protection Agency.[10] The problem is that all government agencies are not created equal. This concentration on domestic regulatory agencies has generated elegant models and arguments about how Congress controls the bureaucracy that turn out to have limited applicability to intelligence. Drawing conclusions from a small and skewed sample of the bureaucratic universe, many Congress scholars make two sweeping claims about congressional control that are not so sweeping after all.

Sweeping Claim #1: Congress Controls the Bureaucracy.   For nearly thirty years now, scholars have argued that Congress controls the bureaucracy, and in surprisingly efficient ways. Barry Weingast, Mathew McCubbins, and others contend that evidence

---

10. Zegart 1999; Ringquist, Worsham, and Eisner 2003. Key oversight work on domestic regulatory agencies includes: Mathew McCubbins, "The Legislative Design of Regulatory Structure," *American Journal of Political Science* 29, no. 4 (1985), pp. 721–48; Terry M. Moe, "The Politics of Bureaucratic Structure." in J.E. Chubb and P.E. Peterson, eds., *Can the Government Govern?* (Washington, DC: Brookings Institution Press, 1989), Weingast and Moran 1983; Mathew D. McCubbins, Roger G. Noll, and Barry R. Weingast [McNollgast], "Administrative Procedures as Instruments of Political Control," *Journal of Law, Economics, & Organization* Vol. 3, No. 2 (Autumn 1987), pp. 243–277. For a call for greater empirical research on congressional control, see John D. Huber and Charles R. Shipan, "The Costs of Control: Legislators, Agencies, and Transaction Costs," *Legislative Studies Quarterly* 25, 1 (February 2000), pp. 25–52.

usually thought to suggest neglected oversight, such as poorly attended congressional committee hearings, actually reveals oversight hard at work.[11] How can this be? According to this literature, savvy legislators hardwire the system to respond to their demands from the start so that they do not have to exert much effort identifying or fixing agency problems later. Much of this research examines how lawmakers craftily ensure that their preferences are heeded from an agency's earliest days. Legislators either build control mechanisms into the very design of government agencies, use (or threaten to use) ongoing controls such as withholding appropriations, or both. The specific mechanisms vary but the logic is the same: government bureaucrats usually respond to legislators' demands because it is in their interests to do so. Agency officials are not stupid. They know, as McCubbins puts it, that "Congress holds the power of life or death in the most elemental terms" for their existence.[12] The mere *anticipation* of possible congressional punishment often makes bureaucrats fall into line. In this world, oversight runs more or less on autopilot. Legislators can make midcourse corrections if necessary, but the beauty of the system is that such interventions are not necessary most of the time, freeing up members of Congress to pay attention to district visits, casework, and other issues that voters care about more.

Note the absence of altruism in this picture. Members of Congress do not have to be woolly-eyed do-gooders to hold government agencies accountable. They only need to be self-interested re-election seekers who want to maximize their political benefits and minimize political costs. These clever politicians are experts at guarding their resources. They build control mechanisms when

11. McCubbins 1985; McCubbins, Noll, and Weingast 1987; McCubbins and Schwartz 1984; Weingast and Moran 1983.
12. McCubbins 1985, p. 728.

designing new agencies from the beginning. They outsource ongoing oversight to third parties whenever they can. And they conduct their own oversight activities only when voters are paying attention and interest groups care the most. The "electoral connection," in David Mayhew's words, makes everything tick.[13] So confident were scholars in the evidence of congressional control that Dan B. Wood and Richard Waterman concluded nearly twenty years ago, "controversy should now end over whether political control occurs. Future research should turn toward exploring the determinants of control."[14]

Strangely, however, this picture of strong oversight bears little resemblance to the realities of U.S. intelligence policy. Between 1947 and 1975, Congress introduced more than two hundred bills to improve intelligence oversight. Only one ever passed.[15] As noted in chapter 2, even after investigations of intelligence scandals during the 1970s led to the establishment of permanent House and Senate oversight committees, actual oversight has continued to struggle. Since the end of the Cold War, seven major initiatives from blue-ribbon commissions,[16] task forces,[17] and even the intelligence committees themselves[18] have found serious oversight weaknesses

13. Mayhew 1974.
14. Dan B. Wood and Richard Waterman, "The Dynamics of Political Control of the Bureaucracy," *American Political Science Review* 85, no. 4 (1991), p. 822.
15. Harry Howe Ransom, "Congress and the Intelligence Agencies," *Proceedings of the Academy of Political Science* Vol. 32, No. 1 (1975), p. 162.
16. Aspin-Brown Commission 1996; Hart-Rudman Commission Phase III Report 2001; *The 9/11 Commission Report: Final Report of the National Commission on the Terrorist Attacks Upon the United States* (New York: W.W. Norton, 2004); *Final Report of the Commission on The Intelligence Capabilities of the United States Regarding Weapons of Mass Destruction* (WMD Commission), 31 March 2005. Accessed at http://govinfo.library.unt.edu/wmd/report/wmd_report.pdf (25 August 2009).
17. Council on Foreign Relations 1996.
18. House Permanent Select Committee on Intelligence, *IC21: The Intelligence Community in the 21st Century* (Washington, DC: GPO 1996); Senate Select Committee on Intelligence, Hearing on Congressional Oversight, 110th Cong., 1st sess., 13 November 2007.

and recommended major reforms to address them. Few of these recommendations have ever been implemented.

For years, in fact, congressional Intelligence Committee chairmen have complained bitterly that intelligence agencies continue to withhold information and flout the committees' intent. In a 2004 report, for example, the House Intelligence Committee revealed that it had repeatedly criticized the CIA's clandestine spying program—called human intelligence or HUMINT by insiders—and recommended corrective action in classified annexes to its annual authorization bills years before 9/11.[19] The committee noted, "After years of trying to convince, suggest, urge, entice, cajole, and pressure CIA to make wide-reaching changes in the way it conducts its HUMINT mission . . . CIA, in the committee's view, continues down a road leading over a proverbial cliff."[20] In 2007, the Senate Intelligence Committee expressed similar frustrations with a range of FBI reform efforts. Noted then-Chairman John D. Rockefeller, "I think there is enormous frustration on this panel, on the Senate Intelligence Committee, about what may or may not be happening in the FBI."[21] It has almost become a ritual for new Intelligence Committee chairmen to demand greater cooperation from the agencies they oversee and vow to rectify the oversight inadequacies of their predecessors.[22]

19. House Permanent Select Committee on Intelligence, *Intelligence Authorization Act for FY 2005*, H. Report 108–558, 108th Cong., 2d sess., 21 June 2004, p. 24.

20. House Permanent Select Committee on Intelligence, *Intelligence Authorization Act for FY 2005*, H. Report 108–558, 108th Cong., 2d sess., 21 June 2004, p. 24.

21. SSCI, Hearing on FBI Strategic Plan, 110th Cong., 1st sess., 23 October 2007.

22. In April 2009, for example, House Intelligence Committee Chairman Silvester Reyes sent an open letter to the CIA and its employees. "One important lesson to me from the CIA's interrogation operations involves congressional oversight," Reyes wrote. "I'm going to examine closely ways in which we can change the law to make our own oversight of CIA more meaningful; I want to move from mere notification to real discussion. Good oversight can lead to a partnership, and that's what I am looking to bring about." Letter from Chairman

This does not sound much like congressional control.

Sweeping Claim #2: Agency Design Can Substitute for Ongoing Oversight. The second sweeping political science claim stems from the first and has to do with the determinants of congressional control. Many scholars argue that Congress keeps bureaucrats in line by building control mechanisms into the original design of agencies. Where an agency is housed organizationally in the executive branch, the administrative procedures it must follow, and the appeals processes third parties such as aggrieved citizens or groups can use to change agency policy or actions are designed to inject congressional preferences and accountability mechanisms into the very structure and routines of agency life. According to this view, congressional control is often front-loaded. Legislators craft core features of agencies at the beginning so they will not have to spend so much energy overseeing them later.[23] Indeed, many assert that agency design and congressional oversight are substitutes. The more that legislators write rules and restrictions into an agency from the start, the less Congress will have to monitor and correct the agency's activities down the line.[24]

Sounds good. The only problem is that this claim is not well-supported by facts or history in the intelligence domain. In the next chapter, I present a wealth of evidence showing that Congress has conducted weak oversight of intelligence agencies, particularly compared to oversight of other policy issues. But—here's the interesting part—Congress *also* failed to build control mechanisms into the CIA when it created the agency in 1947. If ever

Reyes to the director of the CIA dated 29 April 2009. Accessed at http://video1 .washingtontimes.com/video/CIAletter.pdf (21 September 2009), p. 2.

23. McCubbins 1985; McNollgast 1987; Moe 1989; Mathew D. McCubbins and Talbot Page, "The Congressional Foundations of Agency Performance," *Public Choice* Vol. 51, No. 2 (1986), pp. 173–190.

24. Bawn 1995, 1997; David Epstein and Sharyn O'Halloran, "Administrative Procedures, Information, and Agency Discretion," *American Journal of Political Science* Vol. 38, No. 3 (August 1994), pp. 697–722.

we would have expected Congress to bake control measures into a new agency from the get-go to make ongoing oversight easier, it would have been with the CIA. But this never happened.

Instead, the provisions creating the CIA in the National Security Act of 1947 were more of an afterthought.[25] Language proposing a statutory CIA was inserted at the last minute into a massive bill that sought to unify the War and Navy Departments into a single Department of Defense after World War II. The battle over military unification took four years, consumed Congress, and pitted the Army and Navy against each other. So bitter was the conflict that the *New York Times* called it a "brass knuckle fight to the finish."[26] While existing intelligence agencies in the War, Navy, Justice, and State Departments fought vigorously over creating any new intelligence outfit with the word "central" in its name, Congress was too busy with military unification to give the issue much thought. In hearings, legislators in both the House and Senate raised few questions. Discussion of the CIA filled just 29 out of 700 pages in the House committee testimony.[27] When House members decided to list the proposed CIA's functions in greater detail, they simply copied and pasted in existing language from President Harry S. Truman's old executive order establishing the CIA's predecessor, the Central Intelligence Group (CIG).[28] Truman himself wrote that the new law succeeded in "renaming" CIG, implying that the act made no substantive changes to its design or operations at all.[29]

The result was that the CIA provisions of the National Security Act were not carefully and cleverly crafted to build in congressional control. They were hastily drawn up without much of an eye

25. Zegart 1999, pp. 163–84.

26. *New York Times*, 20 October 1945.

27. U.S. House, Committee on Expenditures in the Executive, Departments. *National Security Act of 1947: Hearings on H.R. 2319.* 80th Cong., 1st sess, 1947.

28. Zegart 1999, p. 182.

29. Harry S. Truman, *Memoirs: Years of Trial and Hope*, vol. 2 (Garden City, NY: Doubleday, 1956), pp. 57–58.

to oversight or control at all. The law contained no specific limits on covert action, no oversight briefing requirements, and no forceful oversight mechanisms. Instead, all of the more robust oversight measures we typically think of today—briefings to legislators of classified intelligence activities, notification to Congress when intelligence operatives undertake covert operations, the ban on CIA assassinations of foreign leaders—were add-ons. The only statutory oversight provisions were ones requiring Senate confirmation of the CIA director and prohibiting the CIA director from concurrently serving on active duty in the military.[30]

In sum, the political science literature suggests, usefully, that oversight can be explained by examining electoral motivations, that weak oversight may be inevitable even if it is not desired or intended, and that oversight is likely to be weaker in intelligence than domestic policy issues. The problem is that this literature also contends that Congress by and large oversees the bureaucracy and that Congress uses both agency design and ongoing oversight mechanisms to keep agencies in line. Both of these claims about congressional control turn out to be highly questionable in the case of intelligence.

THE INTELLIGENCE LITERATURE[31]

The intelligence literature suffers from the opposite problem. Where the political science literature makes broad generalizations about effective oversight that apply poorly to intelligence, the intelligence literature has produced in-depth and vivid histories that do not illuminate broader oversight dynamics. Intelligence exceptionalism is a common theme here. Scholars emphasize that intelligence is a policy area unlike any other and therefore not suitable for

30. Zegart 1999.
31. The analysis in this section was developed by Amy Zegart and Julie Quinn, "Congressional Intelligence Oversight: The Electoral Disconnection," *Intelligence and National Security*, Vol. 25, No. 6 (December 2010), pp. 751–54.

social science theorizing.[32] In addition, this literature seeks to explain fluctuations in intelligence oversight over time, not why oversight has remained so problematic for so long. And it focuses on individual personalities and specific events rather than the forces that transcend them. The field is rich with work that compares and contrasts the tenures of various congressional intelligence committee chairmen, dissects the personalities of CIA directors, and assesses the impact of various intelligence scandals. While these are vital contributions to our understanding of intelligence oversight, the net effect is a focus on nuance at the expense of generalizability.

Intelligence research on oversight falls into two camps. The first focuses so much on what makes intelligence policy unique that it fails to focus on oversight commonalities among intelligence and other policy domains or to build on the contributions made by political scientists. Frank J. Smist, for example, highlights the fact that the intelligence committees are "unique creatures of Congress."[33] He develops two oversight "models"—which he calls institutional (supportive) and investigative (challenging)—to characterize the committees' relationships with the Intelligence Community. But in Smist's own words, these models do "not have the very formal sense found in some social science literature." The word "model," Smist notes, "signifies more of an outlook, perspective, or attitude."[34] Although Smist's approach examines in detail how the House and Senate committees have functioned since their creation in the 1970s, it does not tether the analysis to or leverage the theoretical frameworks of the political science literature.

---

32. Smist 1994; Marvin C. Ott, "Partisanship and the Decline of Intelligence Oversight," *International Journal of Intelligence and CounterIntelligence* 16 (2003), pp. 69–94.

33. Ibid., p. 19.

34. Ibid.

Britt Snider also offers an informative description of oversight successes and failures in an aim, as he puts it, to "write something that would help CIA employees better understand the Agency's relationship with Congress."[35] But this, too, is more of a play-by-play narrative of oversight through the ages rather than an explanation of why intelligence oversight looks the way it does. Snider does not offer an explanation of why weak oversight persists despite a changing cast of characters and events over time, a question that has been central to the political science oversight literature for years.

The second camp in the intelligence oversight literature incorporates aspects of the two dominant political science oversight models—dubbed police patrol and fire alarm oversight—but still focuses on historical narrative and the role of individuals rather than the systemic forces that give rise to poor oversight.

David M. Barrett challenges the conventional wisdom that intelligence oversight was absent or weak before the permanent select committees were established in the 1970s. He finds that oversight might not have been comprehensive, but it was far more robust and dynamic during the CIA's first fifteen years than most scholars believe.[36] Interestingly, in his afterword Barrett explicitly discusses the fire alarm oversight model which had become a dominant paradigm in political science. We examine the details of the fire alarm model in the next chapter. Here, it is important to note the basics: the model, developed by Mathew D. McCubbins and Thomas Schwartz in the 1980s, posits that legislators outsource oversight to third parties (namely interest groups) and jump into action themselves with hearings and other measures only when those third parties sound an alarm.[37] Barrett notes

35. Snider 2008, pp. xiv–xv.
36. Barrett 2005, p. 458.
37. McCubbins and Schwartz 1984.

that his historical research does not directly use the fire alarm model, but his findings generally align with it. "McCubbins and Schwartz never mention the CIA," he writes, "but the events described herein mostly fit the pattern they describe."[38]

Although Barrett carefully mines the archival record for new insights and makes an effort to tie intelligence to the broader political science oversight literature, he ends up overlooking that literature's most important contributions. In Barrett's conception, fire alarm oversight is shorthand for saying, "when really bad things happen, Congress reacts in some way." But this is not what McCubbins and Schwartz say. Their point is not that Congress reacts to scandals or mishaps; congressional observers have known that forever. *Their point is that all decisions about congressional oversight are driven by electoral incentives.* Their central proposition is that fire alarm oversight is more attractive than the alternatives because it is electorally more efficient. Legislators outsource alarm-ringing to interest groups and constituents who bear the costs of monitoring and who reward legislators for rectifying problems they care about the most. Congress, in short, designs a system where others do the hard work of monitoring and legislators reap the rewards. This incentive-based analytic framework is McCubbins and Schwartz's most important contribution to the literature, but it makes no appearance in Barrett's work.

Loch K. Johnson makes the greatest effort to incorporate political science oversight models into his analyses, making explicit reference to them in several articles. In one, he argues that "greater devotion" to more centralized, active, and constant oversight activities—the police patrol model—is far preferable in intelligence to "waiting for 'fire alarms' to sound in the night."[39] Why? Because

---

38. Ibid., p. 460.
39. Loch K. Johnson, "The Contemporary Presidency," *Presidential Studies Quarterly* 34 (2004), p. 835.

in the secret world of intelligence, fires are unlikely to be noticed and alarms are unlikely to be rung until after a major scandal or catastrophic failure has already occurred. In another article, Johnson takes this critique of oversight even further, arguing that robust police patrolling of the Intelligence Community by Congress "has been minimal, resulting from the lack of motivation by lawmakers."[40] In a third piece, Johnson argues that a distinct pattern has emerged in intelligence oversight activities since the mid-1970s: "a major intelligence scandal or failure—a shock—converts perfunctory patrolling into a burst of intense firefighting, which is then followed by a period of dedicated patrolling that yields remedial legislation or other reforms designed to curb inappropriate intelligence activities in the future."[41] Johnson claims that both police patrol and the more reactive, sporadic fire alarm oversight models are at work, however insufficient and ineffective the combination may be.

Johnson's work comes closest to bridging the gap, yet still misses a crucial piece of the puzzle. Essentially, his remedy for weak intelligence oversight is to call on legislators to assume their oversight responsibilities with renewed dedication, more gusto, and greater vigilance.[42] Such personal leadership can certainly be important: Johnson notes that a few powerful legislators who are committed to oversight can substantially improve their committee's effectiveness. But the point is that this scenario is highly unlikely.

---

40. Loch K. Johnson, "Congressional Supervision of America's Secret Agencies: The Experience and Legacy of the Church Committee," *Public Administration Review* 64, No. 1 (2004), p. 4.

41. Loch K. Johnson, "Secret Spy Agencies and a Shock Theory of Accountability," University of Georgia Occasional Paper Series, 2006, p. 1.

42. Loch K. Johnson, "Ostriches, Cheerleaders, Skeptics, and Guardians: Role Selection by Congressional Intelligence Overseers," *SAIS Review* XXVIII, No. 1 (2008), pp. 93–108; Loch K. Johnson, "The Contemporary Presidency," *Presidential Studies Quarterly*, 34 (2004), pp. 828–837; Johnson 2004. See also Loch K. Johnson, "The U.S. Congress and the CIA: Monitoring the Dark Side of Government," *Legislative Studies Quarterly*, 5 (1980), pp. 477–499.

Indeed, hanging oversight hopes on the dedication of individual members neglects the very institutional mechanisms and incentives that have created Congress's oversight problems in the first place. Suggesting that individual leadership is the solution to weak intelligence oversight logically implies that individual leadership is also the cause. This analytic approach is the exact opposite of the one that dominates the political science literature. Leaders certainly matter. But in the broader oversight scheme, history suggests that institutional constraints usually matter more.[43]

SUMMARY

Research in political science and intelligence studies captures important but incomplete elements of intelligence oversight dynamics. Political science's focus on oversight writ large identifies the right causal mechanisms but reaches the wrong conclusions. Yes, electoral incentives drive oversight. But—and this is what Congress scholars have largely failed to consider—if the incentives are weak, then control (whether built into an agency's design or determined by subsequent congressional activities) will be weak, too. On the other hand, intelligence scholars are right to suggest that intelligence *is* different in key respects, but wrong to conclude that oversight is explained best by idiosyncratic factors like personalities and events. As we shall see, intelligence is different, but not that different. Secrecy, voter inattention, weak interest groups, and other factors unique to intelligence create powerful, perverse incentives for legislative oversight. But these incentives are enduring, not random or ephemeral. They operate systematically, in ways that can be explained and predicted without having to consider whether Chairman X cares more about intelligence than Chairman Y, whether Republicans or Democrats

---

43. Zegart and Quinn 2010.

are in the majority, or whatever the scandal *du jour* might be. The critical question is not so much whether intelligence is different, but how those differences affect the most fundamental element of legislative politics: re-election prospects. Put simply, Congress has struggled to oversee intelligence for so long because the costs and benefits have never added up for legislators. The same electoral cost-benefit calculations that are so critical to understanding how and why Congress controls the bureaucracy also explain how and why Congress does not control the intelligence bureaucracy.

CHAPTER FOUR

Policemen, Firefighters, and Spooks

How Oversight Varies Across Policy Domains

AMY ZEGART AND JULIE QUINN

As the last chapter notes, political science theories offer some powerful analytics to examine intelligence oversight but fail to take stock of what makes intelligence different. Intelligence studies research, on the other hand, is all about what makes intelligence agencies different, and as a result fails to consider broader oversight dynamics that apply across policy domains. In this chapter, we flesh out more carefully just what is common and what is unique about intelligence agencies by explicitly applying the two most popular oversight models in political science to a range of policy areas.

We start by discussing the claims of the police patrol and fire alarm oversight models. Next we turn from abstract logic to concrete data, exploring the requirements for both models to work by asking two questions: "How would we know robust oversight when we see it?" and "How have these metrics of oversight varied across

An earlier version of this chapter was published as "Congressional Intelligence Oversight: The Electoral Disconnection," *Intelligence and National Security* Vol. 25, No. 6 (December 2010), pp. 744–66, copyright © 2010 Taylor & Francis Ltd./ Routledge, www.taylorandfrancis.com, reprinted by permission of the publisher.

The co-author of this chapter, Julie Quinn, is the founder of QuinnWilliams, a policy research and analysis firm, and previously served as a research associate at the UCLA Luskin School of Public Affairs.

policy domains, including intelligence, over time?" These questions are hard to answer but important.[1] Past work on oversight has focused either on case studies of a single committee[2] or on oversight activities of Congress as a whole.[3] Assessing how oversight varies *across* policy areas and congressional committees has garnered relatively little attention.[4] We seek to begin filling this gap, building on John D. Huber and Charles R. Shipan's call to push the congressional control literature to more precise empirical tests and evidence while at the same time paying special attention to intelligence.[5] Using three original data sets that track congressional committee hearings, legislative productivity, and interest group data from the past twenty years, we find that House and Senate Intelligence Committees have been dramatically less active in their oversight duties compared to other committees. We also find evidence that electoral incentives explain

---

1. As noted in chapter 2, defining and measuring effective oversight is hard because agencies live in a world of contested interests where "good oversight" for one group is seen as poor oversight by another; because agencies typically have conflicting mandates; and because a significant degree of oversight activity is unobservable from the outside. Nevertheless, analyzing formal indicators of Congress's oversight activity levels and how they vary across committees is the industry standard and a useful place to start.

2. See, for example, Weingast and Moran 1983; Terry M. Moe, "An Assessment of the Positive Theory of 'Congressional Dominance.'" *Legislative Studies Quarterly* 12 (November 1987), pp. 475–520.

3. Aberbach 1990; McCubbins and Schwartz 1984; Thomas E. Mann and Norman J. Ornstein, *The Broken Branch: How Congress is Failing America and How to Get It Back on Track* (New York: Oxford University Press, 2006).

4. Ringquist, Worsham, and Eisner (2003) note that Congress is expected to oversee less in policy areas that command low public salience or feature high degrees of complexity. Bawn (1997) finds significant differences in preferences about statutory control between committee members and non-members, with committee members favoring lower statutory controls built into the design of agencies within their jurisdiction, and non-members favoring greater statutory controls. Beyond these more general treatments, however, the literature does not dive deeply into the empirics of how oversight varies across policy issues.

5. John D. Huber and Charles R. Shipan, "The Costs of Control: Legislators, Agencies, and Transaction Costs," *Legislative Studies Quarterly* Vol. 25, No. 1 (2000), pp. 25–52.

why. In short, existing oversight models identify the right root cause, but come to the wrong conclusions: legislators do labor to satisfy the preferences and demands of organized interests and concerned citizens. But that very responsiveness leads Congress to oversee some policy areas more than others. The result is that intelligence has gotten short shrift, even though the national security stakes are high.

POLICE PATROL OVERSIGHT

For years, congressional observers believed that oversight was essentially a continuous, do-it-yourself legislative enterprise. Members and their staffs did the heavy lifting, constantly scanning agency activities for hints of wrongdoing, inefficiency, or violations of legislative goals and priorities. Dubbed "police patrol" oversight, this type of oversight has been characterized by two core features. The first is that it is constant. Congress can never see everything all the time, but by sampling agency activities on a continual basis, the very practice of oversight can catch some problems and deter the emergence of others. The second feature of police patrol oversight is that it is centralized. Legislators and their staffs are the ones who hold hearings, summon agency officials, make inquiries, and demand changes. Perhaps the best-known work in this field is Joel Aberbach's 1990 book, *Keeping a Watchful Eye*. Using composite data from twelve congressional committees, Aberbach finds that vigorous and ongoing police patrol oversight increased from the 1960s to the 1980s.[6] Changes in the composition and size of committee staffs created, in his words, "a surprisingly active approach to keeping track of agency activities."[7]

---

6. Aberbach 1990, pp. 219–230.
7. Ibid., p. 104.

Problematic Assumptions.   Although the police patrol model has been widely viewed as a universal framework, it rests on two assumptions that turn out to be problematic in the intelligence context. The first is that police patrols are assumed to work well just about everywhere. Notably, Aberbach's important study takes the entire Congress as the unit of analysis. Although he gathers committee-level data, Aberbach never presents it, listing instead aggregate oversight data such as the numbers of hearings and meetings held or bills passed per congressional session. His goal is not to examine differences across oversight committees, but to provide an overview of congressional oversight. He finds increasingly active oversight but misses the opportunity to examine whether and how oversight varies in different policy contexts. All congressional committees are assumed to be equal, or at least equal enough so that generalizations about oversight can be made and important disparities between committees left aside.[8] This assumption creates false confidence, suggesting implicitly that the intelligence committees are patrolling just as vigorously as their counterparts. As we discuss below, this is not at all the case.

Second, the police patrol model also assumes that legislators are able to sample agency activities on an ongoing basis in order to detect problems and violations, correct them, and prevent them from recurring. For the entire process to work, however, information about agency activities must be readily available. In the intelligence world, it isn't.

Economists call these kinds of oversight situations **principal-agent problems**.[9] We see them often in everyday life. A car me-

8. Notably, he also does not include intelligence among his committee selections so it is impossible to know whether congressional oversight of the Intelligence Community proved more active, less active, or about the same as Congress's oversight more generally during the same period, a topic we examine more below.

9. Paul Milgrom and John Roberts, *Economics, Organization, and Management* (Englewood Cliffs, NJ: Prentice Hall, 1992).

chanic overcharges because he knows the customer has no idea how to fix the car and cannot monitor the mechanic's work directly. A child says he has walked the family dog when he has not. In these kinds of situations, one party (the principal) must rely on another party (the agent) to carry out a task. The problem is that the principal and agent have divergent interests (the mechanic wants to charge the most he can while the customer wants to pay the least; the parent wants the dog walked, the child would rather play). If the principal cannot directly monitor the agent's activities, or if the principal lacks the knowledge to understand what the agent's work requires, the temptation is strong for the agent to cut corners, overcharge, spend time on something else, or shirk in other ways. Information is the key to mitigating principal-agent problems. The more the principal knows about how to perform the task at hand or about what the agent is actually doing, the less likely it is that the agent will veer off course.

In the oversight context, all of this means that agencies shirk less when their overseers know and monitor more. Information is the most important ingredient in keeping bureaucrats in line. And we know that information about agency activities is much more readily available in the unclassified world than the classified world. Comparing environmental policy to clandestine intelligence collection efforts illustrates the point. In even the most contentious environmental issues, information is plentiful and relatively easy for legislators to acquire. For starters, interest groups abound, bombarding legislators with up-to-the-minute information and analysis about the issues they care about most. In addition, the default setting for the Environmental Protection Agency is to make reports, regulations, and activities publicly available. Even the agency's personnel directory is available online. Finally, no special rooms or secret briefings are needed for legislators to get a handle on the agency's activities.

The intelligence business affords none of these informational benefits to overseers. As we shall see, there are very few interest groups in intelligence compared to other policy areas. Details about secret collection efforts and analytic products are, for obvious reasons, not ordinarily available to the public. But intelligence agencies often do not provide even basic information about their programs, organization, personnel, and budgets to the public— for less obvious reasons. To get even rudimentary information, interested citizens or groups must either comb through public documents for clues or file a Freedom of Information Act request, which can take years to process and often produces no new information at all.[10] Indeed, intelligence information is so

10. In the spring of 2011, for example, I asked the Office of the Director of National Intelligence (ODNI) for a breakdown of analyst attrition rates by agency. Total attrition across the IC was already publicly available, but I was seeking a breakdown by each intelligence agency over a longer period of time. Of particular interest, I noted in my request, was obtaining data that would enable a year-by-year comparison of FBI analyst attrition rates compared to the analyst attrition rates of other IC agencies. The ODNI informed me that I would need to file a Freedom of Information Act request. I did, despite the fact that one former senior intelligence official assured me that the information was not, and should never be, classified. A few weeks later, I received information that I already possessed.

Over-classification also applies to very old records. In 1998, a Freedom of Information lawsuit filed by the nonprofit James Madison Project requested declassification of six World War I documents believed to be the oldest classified documents in U.S. archives. All dated from 1917–1918 and apparently discussed the use of secret ink, including inks that may have been used by the Germans during the war. The CIA refused the request, arguing that "some of the methods described in the documents in question are still used by the CIA, and that third parties inimical to the interests of the United States may not know which of the [invisible ink] formulas are still considered reliable by the CIA and approved for use by its agents." [The James Madison Project vs. National Archives, Case 1:98-cv-02737-TPJ Document 40 Filed 03/05/02, C.A. 98–2737 p. 3. Accessed at http://www.fas.org/sgp/jud/ink -030502.pdf (20 April 2011).] In 2002, a federal court accepted that argument and ruled in favor of the CIA. The CIA finally reversed its own decision and declassified the documents—without explanation—in 2011, nearly a hundred years after they were written. *Secrecy News Web Blog*, Federation of American Scientists Project on Government Secrecy, Volume 2011, Issue No. 37. Accessed at http://www.fas.org/ blog/secrecy/ (20 April 2011). For more on over-classification, see Amy B. Zegart, "Spytainment: The Real Influence of Fake Spies," *International Journal of Intelligence and Counterintelligence*, Vol. 23, No. 4 (2010), pp. 599–622.

tightly restricted, even the CIA's chief public spokesman, George Little, does not post his contact information on the agency's web site. Moreover, legislators cannot do their homework at home. Examining important intelligence issues usually requires traveling to special secure locations (called SCIFs) and at times means hearing classified briefings alone, without the benefit of staff support.

Given these conditions, one would naturally expect to find more shirking in the classified setting than the unclassified one for the simple reason that information is scarce in one and plentiful in the other. The more sources of information available to legislators, the easier it is for them to sample activities in a meaningful way. Indeed, with code word security clearances and tightly compartmentalized activities, intelligence officials often have a difficult time learning what people in their own organization are doing. As Director of National Intelligence James Clapper noted, the list of ultra-secret programs in the Pentagon is so long and their access so restricted, "There's only one entity in the entire universe that has visibility on . . . [them all], that's God."[11] When senior intelligence officials have that hard a time accessing information from the inside, legislators are unlikely to stand a better chance of monitoring their activities from the outside.

FIRE ALARM OVERSIGHT

In contrast to police patrol oversight, fire alarm oversight is less constant, less centralized, and less direct. Driven by criticisms that Congress was not being proactive, McCubbins and Schwartz countered that Congress does not need to oversee all the time to be effective. Instead, McCubbins and Schwartz posit that congressional oversight looks less like police patrolling and more like firefighting:

11. Dana Priest and William M. Arkin, "Top Secret America: A Hidden World, Growing Beyond Control," *Washington Post* Special Report, 19 July 2010.

Congress sets up a system of rules, procedures, and practices that empower citizens, groups, and other third parties to monitor agencies and ring the alarm if they see smoke. Rather than constantly patrolling, Congress springs into action only when concerned third parties are upset enough to sound an alarm. In this fire alarm system, McCubbins and Schwartz contend, Congress only expends effort overseeing agencies when aggrieved parties really care. And because the political landscape is littered with interest groups and attentive constituents, oversight is generally active, enabling Congress to control the bureaucracy.[12]

McCubbins and Schwartz argue that legislators usually prefer the fire alarm model because it provides greater net political benefits. The electoral connection is pivotal. Congressional rules and structures are designed in ways that maximize the re-election interests of individual members.[13] Fire alarm oversight serves this purpose by ensuring that legislators devote their energies to issues that are considered most important to their most important constituents—organized interest groups, whose support is vital to any re-election campaign. Citizens who are concerned and organized enough to ring an alarm are citizens who are likely to get out the vote and provide other campaign support. And because legislators jump into action only when organized interests demand it, they can allocate more time to casework, position taking, and other activities that boost their re-election prospects.

Problematic Assumptions.   Like the police patrol model, McCubbins and Schwartz's fire alarm model rests on four assumptions that turn out to be problematic in the intelligence world.[14]

---

12. McCubbins and Schwartz 1984.
13. Mayhew 1974.
14. The first three assumptions are listed explicitly in McCubbins and Schwartz 1984, pp. 166–67. The fourth assumption about interest groups is implied in their analysis.

They are:

Technological Assumption: There are two forms of congressional oversight: police patrol and fire alarm.

Motivational Assumption: Legislators seek to take as much credit and avoid as much blame for the benefits and costs borne by their constituents.

Institutional Assumption: Federal agencies act as agents of Congress.

Interest Group Assumption: Organized interest groups (and concerned citizens) drive oversight, rewarding legislators for police patrolling and responding to fire alarms.

While all four assumptions seem reasonable for most policy issues, a closer look finds that only the technological assumption actually applies well to intelligence.

The motivational assumption, which posits that legislators seek to take credit for successful policies and avoid blame for ones that hurt their constituents, hinges on the idea that "avoiding blame" and "claiming credit" are relatively straightforward exercises. Members can and do select options and take actions that minimize one and maximize the other. But the relationship between policies and outcomes is much less transparent and much more risky in national security affairs than in most other policy areas. If a legislator argues that education spending should be increased, he is a champion of education whether or not a given bill passes or fails. But if a legislator argues that more money should be spent on Predator drones or tacitly approves a covert CIA action, he may not be regarded as a champion of American security; he may be accused of being a warmonger, a CIA lackey, or both. What's more, as U.S. humanitarian intervention in Somalia, the Iraq War, and the war in Afghanistan illustrate, foreign affairs is filled with crucial votes that look politically popular at one time and politically disastrous later. Most domestic policy issues do not confront nearly the same kind of temporal uncertainty. It is fair to say that legislators can predict with some confidence how their constituents will view a vote for the Children's Health Insurance Program ten years down the line. Decisions that put the American military in harm's way are quite another matter.

The institutional assumption also applies poorly to intelligence. McCubbins and Schwartz contend that federal agencies consider themselves agents of Congress. This is certainly news to America's seventeen federal intelligence agencies. Although intelligence officials do provide information to congressional leaders and committees, they ordinarily do not distribute intelligence products to legislators or consider Congress a primary intelligence "customer." The CIA and its ODNI successor have repeatedly stated that the executive branch is their primary customer.[15] Each morning the Director of National Intelligence delivers a top-secret intelligence briefing to the president and his top national security aides, not Speaker John Boehner, Senate Majority Leader Harry Reid, or anyone else in Congress. Indeed, the President's Daily Brief is so highly classified, rarely has a member of Congress seen it, even years after the fact. What McCubbins and Schwartz assume to be a close institutional connection between Congress and the executive branch is, for intelligence officials, far from it.

Third and finally, the success of fire alarm oversight is tied directly to the presence of interest groups and, to a lesser extent, concerned citizens. McCubbins and Schwartz take the interest group assumption as an article of faith. But if interest groups are not plentiful or powerful, or if secrecy and classification restrictions

---

15. Office of the Director of National Intelligence. *National Intelligence: A Consumer's Guide,* 2009. Accessed at http://www.dni.gov/reports/ic_consumers_guide_2009.pdf (7 July 2010).

make it too difficult for them to detect any smoke, it follows that fire alarm oversight will suffer. As we discuss below, this is precisely what has happened to intelligence oversight.

In sum, both the police patrol and fire alarm models rest on assumptions which render them ill-suited to explaining intelligence oversight. And neither one addresses variance across policy domains. The congressional oversight literature provides general models that turn out to apply poorly to one of the most important policy areas in American politics.

POLICE PATROL REVISITED: WHAT THE DATA SHOW

So much for logic. The next task is to look at the data and ask whether Congress actually does oversee more and differently in some policy areas than others. The answer is a resounding yes.

In order to measure the variance in police patrol oversight across policy domains, we examine the two most commonly used metrics in the literature: legislative productivity and hearing activity. Table 4.1 compares the legislative activity of the Senate Intelligence Committee to three other senate committees: Foreign Relations, Commerce, and Banking. When determining how to select appropriate committees for comparison, we relied on Richard Fenno's classification system which divides congressional committees into three categories: prestige, policy, and constituency committees.[16] Because intelligence is considered a national policy issue, we restricted ourselves to the policy category. In addition,

16. Richard F. Fenno, Jr., *Congressmen in Committees* (Boston: Little, Brown, 1973). Prestige committees are considered the most desirable assignments and include committees such as Appropriations and Ways and Means. Policy committees deal with issues of national importance, including Banking, Finance, Commerce, Foreign Affairs, and Judiciary. Constituency committees serve a critical district need and include Agriculture, Merchant Marine and Fisheries, and Veterans' Affairs, to name a few.

Table 4.1 Legislative Activity Levels of Senate Intelligence vs. Other Policy Committees, 1985, 1990, 1995, 2000, and 2005

Committee	Congress	Year	Number of Bills/ Jt. Resolutions* Considered	Number of Bills/ Jt. Res. that became Law	Legislative Success Rate (%)
Intelligence	109th	2005	9	0	0%
	106th	2000	2	0	0%
	104th	1995	7	2	29%
	101st	1990	9	0	0%
	99th	1985	2	2	100%
	Average		**6**	**1**	**17%**
Foreign	109th	2005	107	6	6%
Relations	106th	2000	122	9	7%
	104th	1995	72	4	6%
	101st	1990	147	29	20%
	99th	1985	142	17	12%
	Average		**118**	**13**	**11%**
Banking	109th	2005	162	16	10%
	106th	2000	148	14	9%
	104th	1995	100	15	15%
	101st	1990	189	22	12%
	99th	1985	205	36	18%
	Average		**161**	**21**	**13%**
Commerce	109th	2005	**	**	**
	106th	2000	241	39	16%
	104th	1995	215	22	10%
	101st	1990	295	43	15%
	99th	1985	214	38	18%
	Average		**241**	**36**	**15%**

*Includes bills and joint resolutions referred to the committee as well as measures originating from the committee.

**This data was unavailable for the Commerce Committee for 2005.

Sources: Intelligence: Report of the Select Committee on Intelligence, Covering the Period 4 January 2005 to 8 December 2006; Special Report of the Select Committee on Intelligence, 6 January 1999 to 15 December 2000; Committee Activities: Special Report of the Select Committee on Intelligence, 4 January 1995 to 3 October 1996; Special Report: Committee Activities of the Select Committee on Intelligence, 3 January 1989 to 28 October 1990; Report of the Select Committee on Intelligence, 1 January 1985 to 31 December 1986. *Foreign Relations*: Legislative Activities Report of the Committee on Foreign Relations for the 109th, 106th, 104th, 101st, and 99th Congresses. *Commerce:* Committee on Commerce, Science and Transportation Legislative Calendar, 106th, 104th, 101st Congresses; Legislative Calendar Report on the Activities of the Committee on Commerce, Science and Transportation, 101st and 99th Congresses. *Banking:* Committee on Banking, Housing, and Urban Affairs Legislative Calendar, 109th, 106th, 104th, 101st, and 99th Congresses.

we took an expansive definition of "legislative productivity," including any bill or joint resolution that either originated in a committee or was referred to a committee and which then went on to become public law.

As Table 4.1 shows, we find that the Senate Intelligence Committee patrols far less than other Senate committees. In 1985, 1990, 1995, 2000, and 2005, the Senate Intelligence Committee considered an average of just six bills or joint resolutions per year. The Senate Foreign Relations Committee, by contrast, considered an annual average of 118. The Banking Committee considered 161 and the Commerce Committee considered a whopping 241 pieces of legislation on average each year. While the Intelligence Committee had an average legislative success rate of 17 percent, which was the highest of all committees, the number reflects the low volume of legislation passing through the committee. On average, the Intelligence Committee produced just one new law per year, compared to thirteen new laws coming out of Foreign Relations, twenty-one from Banking, and thirty-six from Commerce. In three of the five documented years, the Intelligence Committee did not pass a single bill or joint resolution that it considered, making it the only committee of the four posting a zero legislative success rate for a given year.

To be sure, one would expect to find greater legislative activity in policy areas such as commerce or banking, which deal with regulatory issues. But we found that Intelligence ranks low even compared to other non-regulatory committees. Table 4.2 shows the percent of total Senate bills considered by committees over a five-year sample taken between 1985 and 2005. Of the twenty total committees, Intelligence ranked nineteenth, contributing less than half a percent of all Senate bills considered during the sampling period. By contrast, Foreign Relations, another non-regulatory committee, ranked tenth, right in the middle

Table 4.2 Percent of Total Senate Bills Considered by
Committees, 1985, 1990, 1995, 2000, and 2005

Committee	Percent of Total
Finance	28.3%
Judiciary	13.0
Health, Education, and Labor	9.6
Energy and Natural Resources	9.3
Commerce, Science, and Transportation	6.6
Environment	6.1
Governmental Affairs	4.5
Agriculture	4.2
Banking	4.0
Foreign Relations	2.9
Armed Services	2.9
Veterans	2.3
Indian Affairs	1.7
Aging	1.3
Rules and Administration	1.2
Budget	0.9
Small Business	0.6
Appropriations	0.4
Intelligence	0.2
Ethics	0.0

Source: E. Scott Adler and John Wilkerson, Congressional Bills
Project (1985–2005), NSF 00880066 and 00880061.

of the pack, producing nearly 3 percent of all bills considered.
The only committee with a lower productivity rate than Intelligence was the Ethics Committee.[17]

In short, these data suggest that the Intelligence Committee typically expends comparatively little time considering legislation.

17. Table 4.2 also shows that the Fenno policy committees we use as the most relevant comparisons are, in fact, relevant. Two of these three policy-oriented committees fall in the middle of the pack, contributing 4.0 and 2.9 percent of the bills considered by all Senate committees during the period, respectively. By contrast, the highest volume legislative outliers—Finance; Judiciary; Health, Education, and Labor; and Energy and Natural Resources Committees—were not included in our original comparison set.

In theory, this low level of legislative productivity should free up more time for other oversight activities such as holding hearings. Hearings, in fact, lie at the heart of Congressional oversight, offering legislators the opportunity to stake out a public position on an issue, signaling to agencies what issues need to be prioritized, and providing valuable information about agency activities and challenges. In a survey of top congressional staffers, more than 40 percent said that they "keep track of what is going on in the programs and agencies by using information transmitted" in hearings.[18]

But we found relatively low levels of hearing activity in intelligence, even when we considered closed or classified hearings. The data show unequivocally that both the House and Senate Intelligence Committees have consistently held fewer hearings than other committees for the past twenty years.[19] Figure 4.1 illustrates the disparity in the Senate. In 1985, the Intelligence Committee held the fewest hearings by far: twenty-three to be exact. By contrast, the Foreign Relations Committee held 108 hearings, two other committees held more than 90 hearings, and no committee held fewer than 60. This trend continued throughout the twenty-year data set: the Senate Intelligence Committee held the fewest hearings in four of the five years sampled. Even in 2005, in the aftermath of 9/11, the Senate Intelligence Committee held just

18. Aberbach 1990, p. 87.
19. We constructed our own data set rather than using Baumgartner and Jones's Policy Agendas Project data in order to capture and examine more granular level data pertinent to this ongoing project. Our data set, for example, notes whether hearings are classified or unclassified, enabling us to compare the openness of oversight activity levels over time. The Policy Agendas Project does not make this distinction in its hearing data. In addition, our dataset codes for all committee meetings, which include briefings, business meetings, hearings, and other activities, allowing us to compare various types of oversight activities across committees. Finally, the Policy Agendas Project data starts and ends with Congressional Information Service (CIS) abstracts. By covering a narrower set of committees, we were able to go deeper, supplementing CIS abstracts (and cleaning up a sizeable number of CIS coding errors) with more detailed data about hearing topics obtained from the committees' staffs, committee web sites, and committee reports.

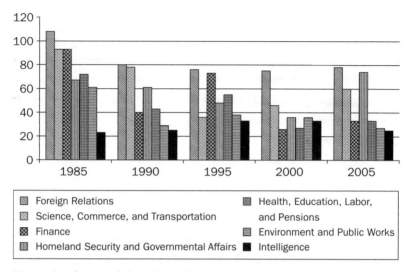

Figure 4.1 Senate Select Committee on Intelligence Consistently Holds Fewer Hearings than Other Senate Commitees, 1985–2005

twenty-five hearings, in either open or closed session, while the Senate Foreign Relations Committee held triple that number.[20]

Figure 4.2 shows that the story is even worse in the House. Even though our data included "closed" intelligence hearings held in classified session, the Intelligence Committee held the fewest hearings in each of the five years sampled. Moreover, the committee never held more than thirty hearings in a given year and averaged just twenty-four hearings per year. The next lowest averages were fifty-five for the Transportation and Infrastructure Committee and sixty-three for the Education and Labor Committee. Foreign Relations and Energy and Commerce averaged more than one hundred annual hearings each.

To guard against the possibility that our five-year sampling

20. It should be noted that our intelligence committee hearing data includes both "open" hearings that are unclassified and "closed" hearings that are held in classified session.

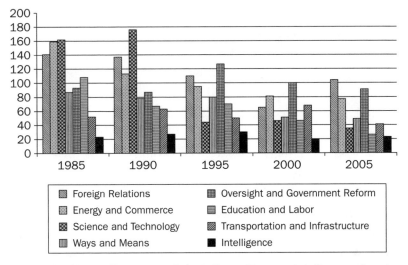

Figure 4.2 House Permanent Select Committee on Intelligence Consistently Holds Fewer Hearings than Other House Commitees, 1985–2005

method missed key intelligence hearing activity in the interim, we also examined intelligence hearings in 2002. Following immediately after the 9/11 attacks, this period was likely to be a high point of congressional intelligence oversight. And yet, even in this tough test, the data confirm the trends we found: namely, lower oversight hearing activity in intelligence compared to other policy areas. Even when we double-count the Joint Inquiry into 9/11 (during which the House and Senate Intelligence Committees held twenty-three joint hearings), the Senate Intelligence Committee held just forty-four hearings throughout 2002.

In sum, legislative productivity and hearing level data do not paint a pretty picture. In the past twenty years, intelligence has grown increasingly important and complicated, with an expanding set of critical policy issues. Indeed, the list of intelligence oversight topics is staggering and growing at an exponential rate. In the 1990s, the core question was how our Soviet-centric intelligence system could transform itself for a new era where weak states posed greater dangers than strong ones and where so many threats—from pandemics to the global economy, terror-ism to climate change—crossed national boundaries in seamless and often unseen ways. After 9/11, an array of new oversight challenges also confronted lawmakers: How and where should suspected terrorists be detained? What interrogation procedures should be used? How could surveillance of electronic communi-cations keep pace with cell phones, fiber optic cables, and other technological changes? What laws should govern the surveil-lance of suspected terrorists in the United States? Should the United States engage in targeted killings, and if so, what are the appropriate procedures to govern the use of Predator drones? Many of these issues raise critical questions such as how to bal-ance security needs with constitutional protections, how to weigh secrecy and accountability, and how to make tradeoffs between process and outcomes. And yet, the data we find shows that Congress still spends more time on other issues.

FIRE ALARM OVERSIGHT REVISITED:
THE ELECTORAL DISCONNECTION

A closer empirical examination also casts doubt on the under-pinnings of the fire alarm model as it applies to intelligence. As noted above, the model hinges on the ability of third parties to monitor agency activities and sound the alarm when necessary. In intelligence, however, these third parties are in short supply.

Three key factors explain the dearth of fire-alarm ringers in in-telligence policy: voters, geography, and interest groups. Ever since the 1950s, political scientists have found that when it comes time to vote, American citizens care far more about domestic than foreign policy issues.[21] In the last twenty years, despite the Soviet

---

21. Gabriel A. Almond, *The American People and Foreign Policy* (New York: Harcourt, Brace, 1950); James N. Rosenau, ed., *Public Opinion and Foreign Policy*

Union's collapse, two wars in Iraq, unprecedented globalization, and the September 11, 2001, terrorist attacks, voters have never listed foreign policy as the most important presidential election issue. In fact, in the 1996 and 2000 elections, foreign policy ranked dead last, below moral values and crime.[22] Congressional elections are even more local affairs. What's more, voter attention to the bureaucratic details of intelligence agencies is naturally low compared to pressing foreign policy issues. Iran's nuclear enrichment is one thing. Database interoperability across U.S. intelligence agencies is quite another. As the House Permanent Select Committee on Intelligence concluded in its 1996 report:

> Intelligence, unlike virtually all other functions of government, has no natural advocates in the public at large. Its direct effect on the lives of most citizens is largely unfelt or unseen; its industrial base is too rarefied to build a large constituency in many areas; it is largely an "inside the Beltway" phenomenon in terms of location, logistics, budget, and concern. The only places where intelligence can hope to find some base level of support are from its Executive Branch masters and its congressional overseers.[23]

(New York: Random House, 1961); Barry Hughes, *The Domestic Content of American Foreign Policy* (San Francisco: W. H. Freeman, 1978); Paul C. Light and Celinda Lake, "The Election: Candidates, Strategies, and Decision" in Michael Nelson, ed., *The Elections of 1984* (Washington, DC: Congressional Quarterly Press, 1985). But note that Aldrich, Sullivan, and Borgida take on this prevailing view, arguing that public attitudes on foreign and defense policy are in fact available and that they influence voters' choices. John A. Aldrich, John L. Sullivan, and Eugene Borgida, "Foreign Affairs and Issue Voting: Do Presidential Candidates 'Waltz Before a Blind Audience?'" *American Political Science Review* 83, No. 1 (March 1989), pp. 123–141.

22. Data from *Los Angeles Times* National Election Day exit polls, 8 November 1988 (Poll #1988–171), 3 November 1992 (Poll #303), 5 November 1996 (Poll #389), 7 November 2000 (Poll #449), 3 November 2004 (Poll #513). Accessed at http://roperweb.ropercenter.uconn.edu/elections/presidential/presidential _election.html (15 August 2009); 2008 exit poll data from CNN. Accessed at http://www.cnn.com/election/2008/results/polls/#USPOOp1 (15 August 2009).

23. House Permanent Select Committee on Intelligence, *IC21: The Intelligence Community in the 21ˢᵗ Century* (Washington, DC: GPO 1996), Section 10.

Geography also provides weak electoral incentives for vigorous intelligence oversight. Because intelligence is a national policy issue and not a regional one, those who care deeply about it are dispersed across congressional districts. This is bad news for oversight. To understand why, one need only compare agriculture policy to intelligence policy. No matter what security threats confront the United States, Congress will always have an overabundance of farm subsidy experts and a shortage of intelligence experts. Why? Because farm interests are clustered in geographic regions with organized interests who provide free information and reward representatives for advocating their positions. Senators James Harlan (R-IA) and Tom Harkin (D-IA) belonged to different political parties and served in different centuries, but both represented Iowa—a fact of life that compelled both men to know a great deal about farming and serve on the Senate Agriculture Committee. Whether these district characteristics lead members to become policy experts[24] or special pleaders for their home industries,[25] the fact is that in most policy areas, geographically concentrated interests incentivize Members to focus on oversight or risk losing their jobs.

Intelligence, by contrast, does not enjoy these electoral connections. Although some surveillance satellite producers are based in certain districts (such as southern California), there is no Iowa equivalent for intelligence, no heavy geographic concentration of industry or natural constituency that encourages legislators to learn the intelligence business and serve on the intelligence committees in order to help the folks back home. Instead, legislators

24. Keith Krehbiel, *Information and Legislative Organization* (Ann Arbor: University of Michigan Press, 1991).
25. Kenneth Shepsle, *The Giant Jigsaw Puzzle* (Chicago: University of Chicago Press, 1978); Barry R. Weingast and William Marshall, "The Industrial Organization of Congress; or, Why Legislatures, Like Firms, Are Not Organized as Markets," *Journal of Political Economy* 96 (1988), pp. 132–163.

have to learn the intelligence business on the job, even though it does little to help them keep their jobs. As the House Permanent Select Committee on Intelligence concluded, service on the committee has "more overt drawbacks than attractions: it likely offers no help vis-à-vis the interests of the Members' districts; it detracts time and attention from issues of direct interest to constituents; and there is little Members can say about what they do."[26] Or as former CIA Director Michael Hayden put it, "No member ever gets a bridge built or a road paved by serving on the Intelligence Committee. It's an act of patriotism."[27]

Finally, intelligence has fewer and weaker interest groups than almost any other policy area.[28] As Table 4.3 shows, in 2008 there were 25,189 registered interest group organizations in Washington. The vast majority of these focused on public interest, business and health related issues. Only 1,101, or 4 percent, were concerned with foreign affairs generally.

An even smaller subset of these was concerned with intelligence policy. To obtain a more precise estimate, we examined all 1,101 foreign affairs–related interest groups and divided them into three categories: those that were likely to be involved with intelligence, those that could possibly be involved with intelligence, and those that were unlikely to be involved in intelligence. Groups that we considered "likely to be involved with intelligence" included the National Counter Intelligence Corps Association, Voices of September 11th, and Terror Free Tomorrow. These totaled 244.

26. HPSCI 1996, Section 10.
27. Interview by author, 19 August 2009.
28. Tracking and measuring the interest group/lobbyist environment is inherently problematic. There are no consensus definitions for the terms "interest group" and "lobbyist" and there are no data sets that capture all organizations. We use Jack L. Walker's broad definition of an interest group and we include both indicators—interest groups and lobbyists—to get the fullest, most complete picture. Jack L. Walker, *Mobilizing Interest Groups in America* (Ann Arbor: University of Michigan Press, 1991).

Table 4.3 Foreign Affairs Interest Groups are
Significantly Less Prevalent than other Interest
Group Types

Issue Area	Groups	Percent of Total
Public Interest	8,456	33.6%
Business	5,418	21.5%
Health	4,701	18.7%
Miscellaneous	2,114	8.4%
U.S. Government	1,729	6.9%
Environment	1,670	6.6%
Foreign Affairs	**1,101**	**4.4%**
Total	25,189	100.0%

Source: Encyclopedia of Associations (Farmington
Hills, MI: Gale, 2008) accessed at: http://galenet.
galegroup.com/servlet/AU/form?!=4&u=n&u=i&u=r&u=
s&locID=lap&n=10 (3 October 2009–18 November
2009).

Groups that were "possibly involved with intelligence" included
the Cold War Veterans Association and United for Peace and Justice and totaled 532.[29] Thus, taking into account those groups
likely or possibly likely to be involved with intelligence, we arrived
at a grand total of 776 groups, or 3 percent of all registered interest
group organizations in Washington.

The policy distribution of registered lobbyists shows a similar
pattern. Figure 4.3 depicts the breakdown of registered lobbyists
by industry from 1998 to 2008. Only 5 percent of all lobbyists
focused on defense issues (which include intelligence policy). By
comparison, all five other sectors had more registered lobbyists—in
some cases, many more. Business lobbyists, with 38 percent of total,
accounted for the largest share. Government-related lobbyists

29. Groups we considered "unlikely to be involved in intelligence" include, for
example, Sister Cities International and Gays and Lesbians in Foreign Affairs
Agencies USA. These totaled 325.

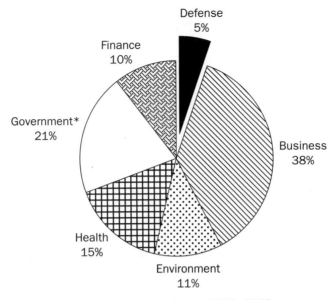

Figure 4.3 Percent of Lobbyists by Industry, 1998–2008

*Government includes issues on the federal, state, and local levels such as education, political parties, and civil service.

Source: http://www.opensecrets.org/lobby/list_indus.php (accessed 26 October 2009).

accounted for 21 percent of the total, health care represented 15 percent of lobbyists, and environmental lobbyists represented 11 percent of the total. Although finance lobbyists represented the second smallest share, they still outnumbered defense lobbyists two to one.

Moreover, if money is any guide, interest groups and lobbyists are not just fewer in intelligence, they are weaker. According to the Center for Responsive Politics, special interests spent more than $23 billion on lobbyists between 1998 and 2008.[30] As Figure 4.4 shows, business lobbying constituted the largest share,

30. Center for Responsive Politics, 2009. Accessed at http://www.opensecrets.org/index.php (26 October 2009).

with 37 percent of total lobbying dollars spent during the ten-year period. Government and health tied for second, each accounting for 16 percent of the total. Although defense contractors are often assumed to be the dominant lobbying industry, defense lobbying represented only five percent of total lobbying spending during the decade. As a subset of defense lobbying, intelligence lobbying accounted for even less.

This weak interest group environment has two major ramifications. First, as noted earlier, many legislators rely on interest groups to keep them informed about agency activities and government programs. Without this steady stream of low-cost information, members have to work harder to learn less. Second, without interest groups pressuring representatives to stay on top of an agency and its activities, the congressman or congresswoman has less motivation to do so. Thus, those serving on the intelligence committees are doubly disadvantaged when it comes to overseeing the agencies' daily activities. They are incentivized to devote their energies to other policy areas and to wait to be notified of an intelligence fire, except that the fire alarm ringers are nowhere to be found.

Earmarks: The Evidence of Absence.   The discussion above may strike some readers as somewhat unsatisfying. This is understandable. Proving the absence of something—in this case, electoral incentives—is never easy. How exactly do we know that voters do not much care about intelligence, that districts do not concentrate groups or industries demanding that legislators pay greater attention to intelligence, or that 244 intelligence interest groups are really so few and weak? One compelling piece of evidence is earmarks. Made famous by the $320 million "bridge to nowhere" for a tiny Alaskan town, earmarks are set-asides put into bills by individual legislators which typically fund pet projects or reward important industries and supporters in their home districts. In other words, earmarks are a tangible manifes-

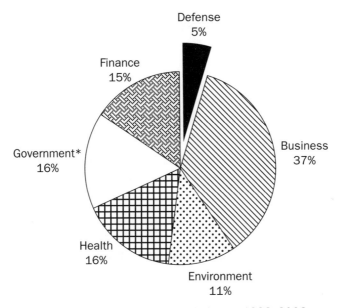

Figure 4.4 Percent of Lobby Spending by Industry, 1998–2008

*Government includes issues on the federal, state, and local levels such as education, political parties, and civil service.

Source: http://www.opensecrets.org/lobby/list_indus.php (accessed 26 October 2009).

tation of all the factors discussed above: voter attention, concentrated geographic interests, and powerful organized groups. The more a particular policy issue draws voter attention, benefits key district industries, or concerns important organized interests, the more plentiful earmarks should be. Similarly, policy areas with lower voter salience, dispersed or limited geographic benefits, and weak interest group attention should garner relatively fewer and lower earmarks. The reasoning is straightforward: Members of Congress deliver benefits to people who notice and reward their effort. Earmarks, in short, provide a useful, albeit indirect, measure of the strength of the electoral connection across policy issues.

For years, intelligence and other national security earmarks were classified. Not anymore. In 2007, after Representative Randy

"Duke" Cunningham's corruption and bribery scandal, Congress required that the purpose, sponsor, and recipient of all earmarks, including classified ones, be made public. Thanks to the nonpartisan group Taxpayers for Common Sense, we now have data that track earmarks in great detail. This important new information shows exactly what we would expect to find: that intelligence earmarks are low on every dimension. Compared to all other policy areas, intelligence earmarks are rarely used, constitute a tiny percent of the intelligence budget, and involve relatively small sums.

As Table 4.4 shows, in FY 2008 congressional earmark spending totaled $39 billion. Unsurprisingly, military construction projects topped the list, with $16.6 billion in set-asides. Other defense projects took second place, with $7.6 billion in earmarks, while energy and water projects ranked third.[31] Intelligence, by contrast, garnered the fewest earmark dollars of any major policy area, with just under $96 million in set-aside funding.[32] These figures are particularly striking when considered against the size of the total federal budget devoted to each policy area. Earmarks constituted more than 15 percent of appropriations for military construction and energy and water projects, but less than .5 percent of the FY 2008 intelligence budget.

In short, earmarks provide further evidence that all of the normal incentives operating in most policy areas are either weak or absent in intelligence oversight. Citizens do not vote based on intelligence issues. There are few, if any, congressional districts with

31. FY 08 Earmarks, The Center for Responsive Politics. Accessed at http://www. opensecrets.org/earmarks/index.php?cyclue=2007&tape=B (4 June 2010).

32. Intelligence ranked second to last in terms of earmark dollars spent overall, but the last place finisher—legislative branch activities—did not constitute a policy area. Note that a quarter of all intelligence earmarked funds went to a $23 million National Drug Intelligence Center located in the district of Appropriations Committee Chairman John Murtha. Richard Willing, "Intelligence Bill's 'earmarks' no longer secret," *USA Today*, 24 May 2007.

Table 4.4 Earkmark Percent of Intelligence vs. Other Budgets, FY 2008

Earmarks by Bill	FY 2008 Earmarks ($ thousands)	FY 2008 Budget ($ thousands)	Earmark % of Budget
Military construction (Veterans Affairs)	16,558,515	84,783,000	19.5%
Energy and Water	6,513,964	36,481,000	17.9%
Interior	972,452	16,825,000	5.8%
Finanical Services (and General Administration)*	1,009,432	20,700,000	4.9%
Transportation and Housing and Urban Dvpt.	3,080,363	114,037,000	2.7%
Commerce, Justice & Science	1,001,064	57,962,000	1.7%
Homeland Security	639,478	40,683,000	1.6%
Defense (excludes intelligence)	7,604,440	547,180,000	1.4%
State, Foreign Operations	189,778	17,505,000	1.1%
Labor, HHS, Education	1,036,516	163,162,000	0.6%
Ag Rural Development	426,503	90,786,000	0.5%
Intelligence	**95,750**	**47,500,000**	**0.2%**
Legislative Branch	1,430	4,429,000	0.0%

Sources: Earmarks from Taxpayers for Common Sense, http://taxpayer.net/search_by_category.php?action=view&proj_id=2789&category=&type=Project (accessed 4 June 2010); Budget figures from Table 3: 2008 Budget Outlays by Agency, U.S. Department of the Treasury, available at: www.treas.gov/press/releases/reports/tableiii.pdf (accessed 4 June 2010). Intelligence budget from ODNI News Release No. 17–08, 28 Oct. 2008 (accessed 21 June 2010).

*Figures from House Appropriations Subcommittee on Financial Services and General Government, Appropriations 2009 bill press release, http://appropriations.house.gov/index.php?option=com_content&view=article&id=268&Itemid=20 (accessed 4 June 2010).

heavy concentrations of intelligence constituencies. Compared to other policy areas, intelligence interest groups are sparse and feeble. These electoral disconnections minimize incentives for legislators to conduct robust oversight in intelligence policy.

SELECTIVE INCENTIVES: THE OVERSIGHT ROAD NOT TAKEN

Intelligence is certainly not the only policy domain where self-interest inhibits the provision of collective goods. As Mayhew concluded, "It is not too much to say that if all members did nothing but pursue their electoral goals, Congress would decay or collapse."[33] Historically, Congress has mitigated this problem by providing "selective incentives"[34]—most notably, in the form of internal power and prestige—to induce some members to work for the greater good. Assignments to "duty" committees such as the Appropriations, Rules, and Ways and Means Committees, which are necessary to make the institution run, are considered the most powerful positions in Congress. As Mayhew writes, "Members are paid in internal currency for engaging in institutionally protective activities that are beyond or even against their own electoral interests."[35]

And yet, in intelligence policy, Congress has not taken the selective incentives route to entice members to serve on the intelligence committees. Instead, Congress has exacerbated the situation by instituting term limits on the intelligence committees but almost nowhere else.[36] More than 90 percent of Congress's committees allow

---

33. Mayhew 1974, p. 140.
34. Olson 1965.
35. Mayhew 1974, p. 146.
36. In the 111th Congress, only five committees mandated term limits: House Intelligence, House and Senate Budget Committees, and the House and Senate

unlimited service so that members can rise in seniority, become more powerful and expert, and provide greater benefits to districts back home. Not the intelligence committees. The House has limited members to four terms since its inception in 1977, and the Senate imposed term limits on members for nearly thirty years, abolishing them only in 2005.[37]

The absence of selective incentives has made the intelligence committees increasingly unattractive assignments. Despite the rising importance of national security and intelligence issues after 9/11, fewer of Congress's most powerful members served on the intelligence committees in 2007 than at any time in the committees' history. In 1987, which was the high water mark, congressional leaders (whom we dub "movers and shakers") constituted 73 percent of the Senate Intelligence Committee and 47 percent of the House Intelligence Committee.[38] By 2007, after two wars in Iraq, and the worst terrorist attacks in American history, that percentage had dropped dramatically, to 33 percent and 25 percent respectively. As the CIA, FBI, NSA, and other intelligence agencies were making front-page news, more of the most powerful members of Congress were turning their attention to other policy matters.

Committees on Standards of Official Conduct. See Guide *to Congress*, 6th ed., Vol. 1 (Washington, DC: CQ Press, 2008).

37. Term limits were abolished in S. Res. 445. See Richard F. Grimmett, *Congressional Research Report* RL33742, "9/11 Commission Recommendations: Implementation Status," 4 December 2006.

38. "Movers and shakers" in the House are defined as: the majority leader, assistant majority leader (whip), minority leader, assistant minority leader (whip), chairmen and ranking members of all committees, and all members of the Appropriations, Rules and Ways and Means Committees. We did not include the Speaker of the House because the Speaker does not ordinarily serve on other committees. Senate "movers and shakers" include the president pro tempore, majority leader, assistant majority leader (whip), minority leader, assistant minority leader (whip), chairmen and ranking members of all standing committees, and all members of the Appropriations Committee.

SUMMARY

Oversight varies in systematic ways for systematic reasons across policy domains. Fire alarm and police patrol models may not apply well to intelligence policy. Their underlying electoral logic, how-ever, does. The electoral connection, which explains why oversight works efficiently in many public policy domains, also explains why there is such weak oversight of intelligence agencies.

CHAPTER FIVE

Oversight Weapons Gone Weak:

Expertise and Budgetary Authority

This chapter moves from comparing oversight across committees to examining more closely what's wrong with intelligence oversight. Delving more deeply into the intelligence committees, I find that Congress's enduring oversight troubles in intelligence stem largely from two institutional deficiencies: limited expertise and weak budgetary power over the Intelligence Community. These weaknesses did not arise by accident. Instead, electoral incentives and institutional prerogatives have led Congress to tie its own hands and block oversight reforms even though the problems are known and the stakes are obviously high. The result is an intelligence oversight system that is rationally designed to serve the re-election interests of individual legislators and protect congressional committee turf but poorly designed to serve the national interest.

EXPERTISE

When it comes to overseeing executive branch agencies, expertise is one of Congress's most powerful weapons, but it is always

An earlier version of this chapter appeared as "The Domestic Politics of Irrational Intelligence Oversight," *Political Science Quarterly* Vol. 126, No. 1 (Spring 2011), pp. 1–26, copyright © 2011 by the Academy of Political Science.

in short supply. As Max Weber noted, bureaucrats always know more about their own agency's activities and policies than the legislators who oversee them. There is something to the old adage that knowledge is power. For congressional overseers, effective oversight requires finding ways to narrow this knowledge gap. The more a committee knows about an agency's policy domain, the better questions it can ask, the more it can monitor agency performance, and the more it can hold the agency accountable. As one congressional staffer put it, "most of what we do in oversight is through the asking of questions."[1] Although oversight has never been easy, developing congressional expertise helps and limiting it hurts.

Broadly speaking, Congress has three ways to develop institutional oversight expertise for any policy. The first is tapping into legislators' homegrown knowledge. Because congressional candidates prefer winning elections to losing them, they have strong incentives to become experts on their districts' key industries before they ever head to Washington and to stay abreast of new developments forever after if they want to keep their jobs.[2]

1. Interview by author, 20 August 2009.

2. Krehbiel argues that Congress rationally and optimally designs the committee system to capitalize on this homegrown expertise, assigning those most informed about a policy domain to the committee in charge of it. This system provides benefits for all, maximizing re-election prospects for individual legislators and providing specialized expertise for Congress as a whole. Shepsle, Weingast, Marshall, and others disagree with this informational story, arguing that committees are stacked with high demanders, not knowledge providers. According to this distributional argument, agriculture committees always favor greater farm subsidies than the House or Senate overall not because committee members know more about subsidies, but because they *need* more subsidies for their constituents back home. Yet the point is that both informational and distributive explanations suggest that committee membership develops and rewards policy expertise; the more legislators know about policy issues affecting important district industries, the better their re-election prospects. Krehbiel 1991; Shepsle 1978; Weingast and Marshall 1988. For an empirical examination of how legislators gravitate to committees that provide special benefits for their districts, see E. Scott Adler, *Why Congressional Reforms Fail* (Chicago: University of Chicago Press, 2002).

The second way that Congress develops institutional oversight expertise is by establishing rules and benefits that foster on-the-job learning. Chief among these are committee membership rules that enable members to serve for unlimited periods of time and develop areas of specialization. Experience and expertise generally go hand in hand. The longer one serves on a committee, the more one is likely to know about its policy issues and processes.

Third and finally, Congress can augment member expertise by developing staff capabilities—either directly by increasing the size of oversight committee and personal staffs, or indirectly through the use of three major congressional support agencies: the Congressional Budget Office, which provides cost estimates for legislation and economic forecasts; the Congressional Research Service, which serves as Congress's reference service; and the Government Accountability Office (GAO), which conducts audits and policy studies of executive branch agencies.

What's Wrong with Intelligence Oversight? All three sources of expertise are far more robust in domestic policy than intelligence. This should not be terribly surprising. Foreign policy in general, and intelligence in particular, has always been considered more of an executive branch affair, for both constitutional and historical reasons.[3] For individual legislators, this arrangement also makes

---

3. Arthur Schlesinger notes that in foreign affairs, more than domestic policy, "Presidents often felt impelled to take action on their own in order to meet threats, real, contrived, or imagined, to the safety of the nation; and here the check-and-balance instrumentalities—not only Congress and the courts but the press and public opinion—were generally less sure of their ground, less confident of their information and judgment, and therefore more inclined to defer to the Executive." Schlesinger in Schlesinger and Bruns 1975, p. xvii. For more, see Aaron Wildavsky, "The Two Presidencies," in *Perspectives on the Presidency*, ed. by Aaron Wildavsky (Boston: Little, Brown, 1975); Louis Henkin, *Foreign Affairs and the Constitution* (Mineola, NY: Foundation Press, 1972); Abraham D. Sofaer, "The Presidency, War, and Foreign Affairs: Practice Under the Framers," *Law and Contemporary Problems* 40, No. 2 (1976), 12–38; Zegart 1999.

electoral sense. The desire to win re-election naturally leads members of Congress to focus on domestic policy issues, which offer greater political benefits and lower political costs. For Congress as a whole, however, these individual incentives weaken the institution's power vis-à-vis the executive branch in intelligence policy.

The Homegrown Expertise Problem: Inattentive Voters, Weak Interest Groups, and Bad Geography. Consider the homegrown expertise of newly elected members. Although legislators come to Washington knowing a great deal about a variety of policy issues, almost nobody walks in the door an intelligence expert. In part, this is because intelligence is a highly technical and cloistered business that requires years of study or insider experience to understand. Of the 535 members of the 111th Congress, only two ever worked in an intelligence agency.[4] This experience base stands in sharp contrast even to the Armed Services Committees, where typically a third of the membership or more has previous military experience.[5] As one congressional intelligence staffer noted, military service may not make a legislator an instant expert on current issues, but "at least they know the rank structure. They can start asking questions. It's like peeling an onion. You start

4. They are Representative Chris Carney (D-PA), who served as an intelligence analyst in the Pentagon, and Representative Mike Rogers (R-MI), who now chairs the House Intelligence Committee and previously spent six years as an FBI agent. Figures from search of biographical directory of the U.S. Congress. Accessed at http://bioguide.congress.gov (22 June 2009).

5. Although Feaver and Kohn find that the number of military veterans serving in Congress has declined sharply since the 1970s, 38 percent of the Senate Armed Services Committee and 32 percent of the House Armed Services Committee in the 11th Congress had prior military experience. Figures based on search of biographical directory of the U.S. Congress. Accessed at http://bioguide.congress.gov (24 August 2009). Peter D. Feaver and Richard H. Kohn, eds. *Soldiers and Civilians: The Civil-Military Gap and American National Security* (Cambridge, MA: John F. Kennedy School of Government, 2001).

with that background and then the questions get sharper." In intelligence, by contrast, the staffer noted, "it would be almost next to impossible to fill the committee with members who have any kind of operational and educational background in intelligence."[6] Instead, understanding intelligence takes the one thing in shortest supply for a legislator: time. As former Senate Intelligence Committee Chairman Bob Graham (D-FL) noted, simply learning the basics usually "exhausts half" of a member's eight-year term on the Intelligence Committee.[7] Former Senate Majority Leader Trent Lott (R-MS) concurred. "There is a huge learning curve to fully comprehend how the nation's intelligence capabilities are being deployed," Lott remarked in the Senate in 2004. "There are very complex technological issues associated with international intelligence and Senators often do not have the time to develop expertise in understanding all of these systems. And that makes it difficult for all committee members to engage in effective oversight."[8]

Admittedly, many policy areas are complicated and hard to understand from the outside. Only intelligence, however, couples this inherent complexity with the trifecta of inattentive voters, weak interest groups, and bad geography. These enduring features of the political landscape turn out to be daunting barriers to developing expertise.

For several decades, political scientists have found that American voters care much more about domestic than foreign policy issues.[9] As we discussed in the last chapter, voters have never listed foreign policy as the most important presidential election issue

6. Interview by author, 20 August 2009.

7. Senator Robert Graham, statement in the *Congressional Record*, 108th Cong., 2d sess., 7 October 2004, p. S10639.

8. Remarks by Senator Trent Lott, Senate Res. 445, *Congressional Record* p. S10265, 1 October 2004. Accessed at http://frwebgate.access.gpo.gov/cgi-bin/getpage.cgi?dbname=2004_record&page=S10265&position=all (17 July 2010).

9. Almond, 1950; Rosenau, 1961; Hughes 1978; Light and Lake 1985.

in the last twenty years, and in fact rated foreign policy last among the issues influencing their presidential votes in 1996 and 2000.[10] Congressional elections are even more locally oriented. As one Congressman bluntly remarked, "My constituents back home don't care how I vote on Bosnia."[11]

Analysis of interest groups shows a similar, striking disparity between domestic and foreign policy. As I discussed in the last chapter, only 4 percent of all interest groups registered in 2008 were concerned with foreign policy. Intelligence-related interest groups were even fewer.[12] And even defense contractors, which are normally thought to be among the most powerful lobbies, spend less money than many domestic policy groups, including the American Hospital Association and AARP.[13]

That's foreign policy writ large. Intelligence policy attracts even less voter attention and weaker interest group support because the key issues are secret, less tangible, more bureaucratic, and not as obviously connected to American national security. Classification plays a major role in limiting the influence and activities even among major intelligence equipment manufacturers. Defense contractors can lobby publicly and vigorously for big-ticket defense weapons programs such as the $28 billion F-22 fighter plane or the $40 billion aerial refueling tanker program.[14] Not

10. Data from *Los Angeles Times* National Election Day exit polls, 8 November 1988 (Poll #1988–171), 3 November 1992 (Poll #303), 5 November 1996 (Poll #389), 7 November 2000 (Poll #449), 3 November 2004 (Poll #513). Accessed at http://roperweb.ropercenter.uconn.edu/elections/presidential/presidential _election.html (15 August 2009); 2008 exit poll data from CNN. Accessed at http://www.cnn.com/election/2008/results/polls/#USPOOp1 (15 August 2009).

11. Interview by author, 2 August 1995.

12. *Encyclopedia of Associations* (Farmington Hills, MI: Gale, 2008). Accessed at http://galenet.galegroup.com/ (18 November 2009). Analysis by author.

13. Center for Responsive Politics Top Spenders 1998–2010. Accessed at http://www.opensecrets.org/lobby/top.php?indexType=a (23 June 2010).

14. Christopher Drew, "Obama Wins Crucial Senate Vote on F-22," *New York Times*, 21 July 2009; Leslie Wayne, "U.S.-Europe Team Beats Out Boeing on Big Contract," *New York Times*, 1 March 2008.

so with major intelligence satellite programs, which are highly classified. As one former Senate Intelligence Committee staffer noted, "The F-22, the tanker, it's all in the open. There's lobbying in intelligence, but it's nowhere near as much. And it's all behind closed doors."[15] Nor can legislators with intelligence satellite manufacturers in their districts talk much about it. Another congressional staffer noted that "legislators can't go and hold intelligence awareness fundraisers in the district."[16]

In addition, as noted earlier, voter attention to the bureaucratic details of intelligence agencies is naturally low compared to pressing foreign policy issues such as the war in Afghanistan or the Israeli-Palestinian peace process. Finally, geography works against aligning electoral incentives to develop intelligence expertise from the start. Because intelligence is a national policy issue and not a regional one, those citizens and groups who care deeply about it are dispersed rather than concentrated in one or a handful of congressional districts. This dispersion further weakens the electoral connection. For many other policy areas, geographically concentrated constituencies provide a self-reinforcing system to develop legislative expertise. Intelligence does not have this advantage.

For all of these reasons, expertise does not arise naturally in intelligence. Although legislators may have strong personal policy interests,[17] they know their time is precious and must be employed judiciously to win re-election.[18] All things being equal, legislators are more likely to develop expertise on issues their constituents care about most and where interest groups are powerful and plentiful.

15. Interview by author, 19 August 2009.

16. Interview by author, 20 August 2009.

17. Richard F. Fenno, Jr., *Home Style: House Members in Their Districts* (New York: HarperCollins, 1978).

18. Morris Fiorina, *Congress: Keystone of the Washington Establishment* (New Haven: Yale University Press, 1989); Mayhew 1974.

Term Limits and On-the-Job Learning. The second route for developing congressional expertise, on-the-job learning, has proven equally challenging. The same electoral incentives that discourage members from joining intelligence committees in the first place also encourage them to leave quickly. Indeed, Congress has designed its own committee rules to ensure this happens in intelligence but almost nowhere else. Nearly all of Congress's committees allow unlimited service, which enables members to develop policy expertise.[19] But the intelligence committees do not. Instead, the House Permanent Select Committee on Intelligence has limited members to four terms since its inception in 1977,[20] and the Senate imposed term limits on members of the Select Committee on Intelligence until 2005.[21] Notably, these committee term limits are not determined by law, but by internal House and Senate rules which are far easier to change.

Many contend that intelligence committee term limits were designed originally to keep legislators from being co-opted by the agencies they oversaw. But that logic has never been applied to the armed services committees or most of Congress's other committees, which face similar co-optation challenges. Moreover, intelligence committee term limits have persisted for years despite repeated calls to abolish them. In 1984, when the Senate's first term limit deadline arose, Senator Barry Goldwater (R-Arizona) grew

---

19. There were fifty-two committees in the 111th Congress, only five of which mandated term limits for membership: House Intelligence, House and Senate Budget Committees, House and Senate Committees on Standards of Official Conduct. See *Guide to Congress*, 6th ed., Vol. 1 (Washington, DC: CQ Press, 2008).

20. Originally, term limits applied even to the Intelligence Committee chairman. However, House rules have since been modified to allow unlimited service by the chair and ranking member. See *Congressional Quarterly Document* g2c6e1–972–36483–1842274. Accessed at http://www.library.cqpress.com/congress/ g2c6e1–972–36483–1842274 (22 May 2009).

21. Term limits were abolished in S. Res. 445. See Richard F. Grimmett, *Congressional Research Service Report* RL33742, "9/11 Commission Recommendations: Implementation Status," 4 December 2006.

so concerned that nine of the committee's ten members would have to rotate off the committee, he tried to get the Senate rule changed. But Goldwater could not convince enough other senators to agree and dropped the issue. During the 1990s, three nonpartisan, major reports on intelligence reform recommended strengthening expertise by ending intelligence committee term limits, including one issued by the House Intelligence Committee's own staff.[22] None of them succeeded fully. Although the Senate finally abolished term limits after using them for nearly thirty years, the House still has them.

A more compelling explanation is that term limits are electorally efficient, ensuring that members can quickly roll off the intelligence committees and onto committees that confer greater benefits to constituents. Serving on the intelligence committees is not a particularly attractive assignment. Data show that Congress's most powerful members have been avoiding the intelligence committees in increasing numbers, suggesting that the intelligence committees are actually *less* attractive now than they were twenty years ago. Table 5.1 tracks the percentage of Congress's most powerful members, dubbed "movers and shakers," who have served on the intelligence committees from the 1970s to the present. In 1987, 73 percent of the members of the Senate Intelligence Committee also held top leadership posts in the chamber, a strong indicator of the importance of the committee. Yet by 2007, only 33 percent of committee members could be classified as "movers and shakers" in the Senate. The percentage of movers and shakers serving on the House Intelligence Committee also fell, from a high point of 47 percent in 1987 to its lowest point—just 25 percent—in 2007.[23]

22. These were the Aspin-Brown Commission 1996; the Council on Foreign Relations 1996; and HPSCI 1996.

23. "Movers and shakers" in the Senate are defined as: the president pro tempore, majority leader, assistant majority leader (whip), minority leader, assistant

Table 5.1 Decline in Movers and Shakers Serving on Intelligence Committees, 1977–2007

Committee	Year	Number of Movers and Shakers	Committee Size	Movers and Shakers % of Committee Total
Senate Intelligence	1977	6	17	35%
	1987	11	15	73%
	1997	9	19	47%
	2007	5	15	33%
House Intelligence	1978*	6	13	46%
	1987	8	17	47%
	1997	7	16	44%
	2007	5	20	25%

*Data not available for 1977.

Source: 1977, 1978, 1987 data from Charles Brownson, *Congressional Staff Directory* (Mt. Vernon, VA: Congress); 1997 data from Joel Treese, *1997 Congressional Staff Directory*, Fall (Alexandria, VA: CQ Staff Directories, 1997); 2007 data from *Congressional Directory: 110th Congress* (Washington, DC: GPO, January 2007).

To be sure, the committee is still very attractive to some. Legislators with presidential aspirations know they can burnish their national security credentials by serving on Intelligence. Some find the world of espionage important and interesting. For a few others, "it's just cool," as one staffer put it.[24] But for most members, overseeing intelligence is both difficult and costly. It requires delving

---

minority leader (whip), chairmen and ranking members of all standing committees, and all members of the Appropriations Committee. House "movers and shakers" consist of the majority leader, assistant majority leader (whip), minority leader, assistant minority leader (whip), chairmen and ranking members of all standing committees and all members of the Appropriations, Rules, and Ways and Means Committees, The Speaker of the House is not included because the Speaker does not ordinarily serve on committees.

24. Interview by author, 28 April 2011.

into highly technical issues without watchdog groups or any of the other information sources freely available in the unclassified world. Legislators cannot even talk about their committee work with constituents.

In sum, the costs and benefits of service on the intelligence committees make term limits an electoral godsend, ensuring that legislators can switch quickly to more attractive committee assignments even though doing so hinders Congress from developing intelligence oversight expertise.

The Expertise Gap. Not surprisingly, term limits have created substantial experience gaps between the intelligence committees and Congress's other oversight committees. Figure 5.1 shows the proportion of "long-termers"—defined as legislators who served five congressional sessions or more—on the Senate Armed Services, Banking, and Intelligence Committees from 1975 to 2008. Note that the Senate Intelligence Committee had half as many long-termers as the other two committees. While 31 percent of the Banking Committee and 30 percent of the Armed Services Committee served at least five congressional sessions, just 15 percent of the Intelligence Committee served that long.

The experience gap is even more pronounced in the House. Long-termers constituted 32 percent of the House Armed Services Committee and 23 percent of the House Banking Committee, but just 5 percent of the House Permanent Select Committee on Intelligence.

Other metrics paint an even starker picture. The longest serving member of the House Armed Services Committee spent fifteen terms, or thirty years, on the committee. A dozen other representatives served twenty years or more. In Intelligence, by contrast, the longest-serving member spent twelve years on the committee, and the majority of legislators spent four years or

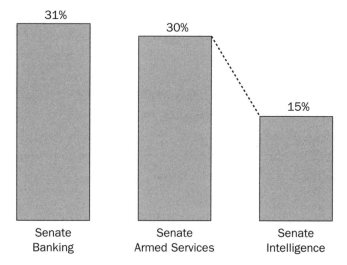

Figure 5.1 Percent of Long-Termers* Serving on Senate Banking, Armed Services, and Intelligence Committees, 1975–2008

*Long-termers are defined as Members serving on the committee five congressional sessions (ten years) or longer.

Source: Official Congressional Directory, 94th–110th Congress (Washington, DC: GPO).

less.[25] In the 103rd Congress (1993–1995), one of the House Intelligence Committee's highest turnover periods, eleven of nineteen members, or nearly two-thirds, were brand new to the committee.[26] The Senate experienced a similar rate of turnover during that time. As one Senate Intelligence Committee staff member who served during the 1990s reflected, "Everyone who was on the committee for the 1993 Word Trade Center attack was gone by

25. The experience gap is probably greater than these figures suggest because the data set does not consider any committee service prior to 1975, when the Armed Services and Banking Committees existed but the Intelligence Committees did not. Thus, members that may appear to have served four terms or less on the congressional Armed Services and Banking Committees actually may have served substantially longer.

26. *Congressional Directory of the 102nd Congress* (Washington, DC: GPO, 1991), p. 491; *Congressional Directory of the 103rd Congress* (Washington, DC: GPO, 1993), p. 477.

9/11." The effect, he said, was that "Nobody had much of a memory, either on the committee or the staff."[27]

Even though 9/11 and the Iraq War have made clear the critical importance of intelligence and exposed the dangers of intelligence weaknesses during the past decade, turnover continues to hinder the development of institutional memory on the congressional intelligence committees. In the 111th Congress, eight of the House Intelligence Committee's twenty-two members, or 36 percent, were brand new to the committee.[28] "Term limits are stupid," noted former CIA Director Michael Hayden. "I don't know why they still have them, but they are hanging themselves."[29]

Outsourcing to Staff: Reining in Watchdogs.   Congressional staff capabilities offer a third mechanism for developing institutional expertise. Yet, the data suggest that Congress has not deployed staff capabilities to compensate for members' expertise limitations. The Government Accountability Office (GAO) has been called "Congress's watchdog" and is widely considered one of the institution's most potent oversight tools, evaluating, investigating, and recommending management improvements to federal agencies. Yet at the insistence of intelligence agencies and the

27. Interview by author, 26 October 2005.

28. Prior service on the intelligence committees was determined by examining congressional directories from the 100th Congress, when the longest-serving representative joining the Intelligence Committee was first elected, to the present. *Congressional Directory of the 111th Congress*, p. 453; *Congressional Directory of the 110th Congress*, p. 443; *Congressional Directory of the 109th Congress*, p. 445; *Congressional Directory of the 108th Congress*, p. 437; *Congressional Directory of the 107th Congress*, p. 441; *Congressional Directory of the 106th Congress*, p. 433; *Congressional Directory of the 105th Congress*, p. 447. All accessed at http://www.gpoaccess.gov/cdirectory/browse-cd-05.html (14 May 2010). Directories for the 100th to 104th Congresses are not available online: *Congressional Directory of the 104th Congress*, p. 426; *Congressional Directory of the 103rd Congress*, p. 477; *Congressional Directory of the 102nd Congress*, p. 491; *Congressional Directory of the 101st Congress*, p. 426; *Congressional Directory of the 100th Congress*, p. 556.

29. Interview by author, 19 August 2009.

U.S. Justice Department, GAO has been prohibited from auditing the CIA and many other intelligence agencies for more than forty years, even though one thousand GAO employees currently hold Top Secret security clearances, seventy-three of whom hold SCI ("Sensitive Compartmented Information") clearances which would grant them access to the most sensitive intelligence information.[30] Since 9/11, several congressional bills to grant GAO stronger intelligence auditing authority have failed. The most recent of these efforts, the 2010 Intelligence Authorization Bill, succeeded only marginally. The bill makes robust GAO auditing theoretically possible but unlikely by placing responsibility for determining GAO's role in the hands of the Director of National Intelligence.[31]

As for strengthening committee staffs, Tables 5.2 and 5.3 show little progress in the House and regression in the Senate. On the House side, the number of staffers has grown in the intelligence committee but continues to lag behind staffing levels in the armed services and banking committees—despite dramatic changes in

30. Post-hearing letter from GAO Comptroller to Senator Daniel Akaka dated 11 March 2008, in Hearing before the Subcommittee on Oversight of Government Management, the Federal Work Force, and the District of Columbia, Senate Committee on Homeland Security and Governmental Affairs, 110th Cong., 2d sess., 29 February 2008, p. 148. It should be noted that GAO has done work for intelligence agencies in the Department of Defense and according to a 1 July 2010 Defense Department directive, GAO currently has access to the Pentagon's most tightly classified programs, including intelligence programs, under certain conditions. For a copy of DoD Directive 5205.07, see http://www.fas.org/irp/doddir/dod/d5205_07.pdf (accessed 7 July 2010).

31. In the spring of 2011, DNI James Clapper issued a directive mandating that all IC components work with GAO. However, the directive also included language that could be interpreted to exclude meaningful GAO auditing—by, for example, making clear that GAO would generally not be allowed to investigate "core national intelligence capabilities or activities." *Comptroller General Access to Intelligence Community Information*, Intelligence Community Directive #114 (Issued 29 April 2011, Effective 30 June 2011), accessed at http://www.fas.org/irp/dni/icd/icd-114.pdf (20 July 2011). For more on GAO and intelligence oversight, see Frederick M. Kaiser, "Congressional Oversight of Intelligence: Current Structure and Alternatives," *Congressional Research Service Report* RL32525, 25 August 2010, pp.22–27.

Table 5.2 House Committee Staff Levels, 1977–2007

	1977	1987	1997	2007	% Change 1977–2007
Armed Services	40	61	55	53	33%
Banking	51	74	58	43	−16%
Intelligence	23	17	24	39	70%

Source: Congressional Staff Directory, 5th–80th editions (1976 to summer 2007), Mt. Vernon, VA: Congressional Quarterly Press.

the intelligence mission, wrenching reform efforts inside the Intelligence Community, and a doubling of the intelligence budget during the past ten years.[32]

On the Senate side, intelligence committee staffs have actually shrunk over time. Table 5.3 shows that staff levels on the Senate Select Committee on Intelligence declined by 15 percent from 1977 to 2007, while the Senate Armed Services Committee Staff ballooned by 59 percent and the Senate Banking Committee staff stayed roughly the same.

As Steven Aftergood concluded, the Intelligence Community has experienced "an extraordinary rate of growth . . . which has not been matched by a comparable increase in the size of the oversight committee staffs or a corresponding expansion of other oversight mechanisms." The overall effect, he told Congress, was

32. As Steven Aftergood notes, the declassified FY 1997 budget for all U.S. intelligence spending was $26.6 billion. The FY 2007 declassified budget for the national intelligence program alone was $43.5 billion. Together with spending for the military intelligence program, which is estimated to be greater than $10 billion annually, the aggregate figure comes to more than $50 billion per year. Statement of Steven Aftergood, Federation of American Scientists, Before the Subcommittee on Oversight of Government Management, The Federal Workforce, and the District of Columbia Of the Committee on Homeland Security and Governmental Affairs United States Senate Hearing on Government-wide Intelligence Community Management Reforms, 110th Cong., 2d sess., 29 February 2008.

Table 5.3 Senate Committee Staff Levels, 1977–2007

	1977	1987	1997	2007	% Change 1977–2007
Armed Services	32	54	59	51	59%
Banking	46	40	37	47	2%
Intelligence	40	38	30	34	−15%

Source: Congressional Staff Directory, 5th–80th editions (1976 to summer 2007), Mt. Vernon, VA: Congressional Quarterly Press.

that there has been "a *net decrease in intelligence oversight*" (emphasis his).[33]

BUDGETARY POWER

Budgetary authority is a second powerful oversight weapon. Students of American government have long recognized the central role that Congress's budgetary authority plays in influencing

33. Ibid. It is important to distinguish between intelligence oversight, which is perennially weak, and homeland security oversight, which appears to have grown overly burdensome. A 17 May 2011 Associated Press story noted that oversight of the Department of Homeland Security (DHS) had grown so onerous, it was overwhelming the department. In 2004, the 9/11 Commission found that 88 different congressional committees and subcommittees were responsible for overseeing homeland security efforts in some way. The commission recommended cutting oversight down to a single point of review. Today, however, the number of congressional subcommittees and committees overseeing the department has grown to 108. (Associated Press, accessed at http://www.washingtonpost.com/politics/inside -washington-for-homeland-security-department-too-much-of-a-good-thing/2011/ 05/17/AFoPjV5G_story.html 17 May 2011). Although DHS is part of the U.S. Intelligence Community, it is a very small part, housing only two of the seventeen agencies that collect and analyze intelligence. The department's intelligence office is tiny compared to many other intelligence agencies and is widely regarded as the weakest in the federal government, with no power to collect or task other agencies with intelligence collection. The FBI, not DHS, has primary responsibility for the domestic intelligence mission. The FBI is also the lead agency for investigating and prosecuting terrorists inside the country. The bulk of DHS activities, by contrast, focuses on hardening targets; presenting "one face at the border" by consolidating the inspection of goods, services, and people entering the United States; and responding to natural and manmade disasters.

administrative agency priorities and activities.[34] Lee Hamilton bluntly noted, "All of us have to live by the golden rule, and the golden rule is that he who controls the gold makes the rules."[35]

Vested in Article I, Section 9 of the Constitution, Congress's budgetary power has been interpreted since colonial days as a two-step process: Congress first authorizes an agency or program and then funds the agency or program through separate appropriations legislation.[36] Generally speaking, oversight in all matters is divided between those who examine agency activities and those who fund them. Most congressional committees are authorizing committees, charged with examining the policies and activities of specific agencies within their jurisdiction. Appropriations of funds are handled exclusively by twelve subcommittees of the House and Senate Appropriations Committees. The system is supposed to ensure that one set of committees develops policy expertise and examines substantive issues in depth, while another set of committees develops fiscal expertise and guards against excessive government spending. But this bifurcated oversight system also ensures that an authorizing committee's budgetary power goes only so far; authorizers can threaten to cut budgets, but appropriators must deliver. Wielding the power of the purse effectively requires coordinating efforts across committees.

In theory, two factors should make coordination easier: availability of information and lower committee workloads. It stands to reason that the more that information is easily available, and the more manageable the budget workload, the easier it is for

34. See, for example, McCubbins 1985.
35. Lee Hamilton, testimony before SSCI, Hearing on Congressional Oversight, 110th Cong., 1st session, 13 November 2007.
36. For more on congressional authorizations and appropriations, see James V. Saturno, "The Separation of Authorizations and Appropriations: A Review of the Historical Record," *Congressional Research Service*, testimony before SSCI, 13 November 2007; Richard A. Best, Jr., "Intelligence Authorization Legislation: Status and Challenges," *Congressional Research Service Report* R40240, 24 February 2009.

legislators and their staffs to deal with issues and work across committee lines. It turns out that committees in other policy areas enjoy both of these advantages far more than intelligence committees do.

Availability of Information. For most policy issues, budget information is widely and publicly available. In the unclassified world, legislators, their staffs, lobbyists, reporters, and citizens all can access detailed budget information with relatively little effort. This means that if an authorizing committee wants to punish an agency by recommending budgetary cuts, everyone knows it. That fact alone enhances the credibility of the threat. To be sure, the availability of information enables many players, including organized interests, to jump into the fray and lobby on behalf of pet programs or agencies. But this informational environment also limits the degree to which an agency can circumvent the authorizing committee and go straight to the appropriations subcommittee without getting punished. As one congressional staffer put it, "If John McCain [who serves as the ranking member on the Senate Armed Services Committee] doesn't like something in the defense appropriations bill, he can object on the floor of the Senate and offer amendments. It's all in the open." The more that information is out in the open, the harder it is for an agency to get away with gaming the system.[37]

Intelligence is a different world. Intelligence budgets are highly classified and closely held. For decades, the executive branch refused to declassify any budget-related information, including total intelligence spending. Today, little more than the top-line figure is declassified, and by law the president can choose to waive declas-

37. Weingast and Moran's important article on congressional control over the Federal Trade Commission does not even look at appropriations subcommittees. Instead, they track how changes in the Senate Commerce Committee led to dramatic changes in FTC policy. Weingast and Moran 1983.

sification if he chooses. Although legislators serving on the intelligence committees and the defense appropriations subcommittees (which handle the intelligence budget) can gain access to this information, anyone else, including personal congressional staffers, cannot. Very few personal staffers (as distinguished from committee staffers) to representatives and senators hold security clearances. In nearly all cases, these clearances are only Top Secret, lower than the Sensitive Compartmented Information (SCI) level required for much of the intelligence committees' work. In the Senate, even clearances are not enough: Senate rules designate Intelligence Committee information "committee sensitive," and prohibit committee staff from sharing information with senators' personal staff even if they hold the appropriate clearances. In addition, members of Congress must read classified documents in a secure location, making it logistically harder for them to do their homework. Many do not. One intelligence staffer estimated that "less than 50 percent of the members will come in and read materials."[38]

These and other secrecy rules are designed to protect highly sensitive intelligence sources and methods. But they also make end runs around the intelligence committees more likely because they give the executive branch a tremendous informational advantage. In the classified intelligence world, where information is tightly restricted and security breaches are serious business, where interest groups are few and weak, and where press reporting is difficult, it is much harder for one congressional committee to know or object publicly to what another committee is doing. As one congressional staff member put it, "There's lobbying in intelligence, but not nearly as much and it's all done behind closed doors . . . What are you going to do if you're an authorizer who doesn't like what's in the appropriations bill? Hold up the entire defense appropriations bill? No way. There's not much recourse for intelligence authorizers,

38. Interview by author, 20 August 2009.

but there is in other areas."[39] Savvy intelligence officials know this, and quietly appeal to appropriators when intelligence committees threaten to cancel or decrease funding for a program. Secrecy creates an environment that is ripe for gaming.

Budget Workloads. Budget workloads exacerbate these problems. Table 5.4 shows the number of legislators, professional staff, and budget responsibilities for each of the Senate's twelve appropriations subcommittees. As the table illustrates, the Defense Subcommittee, which is responsible for the intelligence budget, has the heaviest workload by far, handling more than half a trillion dollars in annual discretionary spending. No other subcommittee comes close. On a per capita basis, legislators assigned to the Defense Subcommittee are responsible for appropriating $33.5 billion of the federal budget each year. That is nearly triple the workload of the Labor, Health and Human Services, and Education Subcommittee, which ranks second; nearly six times greater than the Veterans Affairs Subcommittee, which ranks third; and roughly ten times greater than the per capita budget workload of the other nine Senate appropriations subcommittees. Similar disparities exist in the House. The per capita budget workload for Defense Subcommittee members is $39.8 billion, four times greater than the per capita budget purview of the second-ranked Labor, Health and Human Services, and Education Subcommittee.[40]

Professional staff capabilities do not compensate much for these disproportionate workloads. Even though the Defense Subcommittee has the largest professional staff of any Senate appro-

39. Interview by author, 19 August 2009.
40. Budget figures from House Appropriations Subcommittee Press Releases Summarizing FY 2010 Appropriations, issued 1 June–30 July 2009, available at http://appropriations.house.gov (accessed 13 August 2009); number of professional staff and legislators on subcommittees from *Roll Call*, available at http://www.congress.org/congressorg/directory/committees.tt?commid=sappr (accessed 13 August 2009).

Table 5.4 Senate Appropriations Subcommittee Budget Workload, FY 2010

Senate Appropriations Subcommittee	Number of Professional Staff	Number of Legislators	FY 2010 Discretionary Budget ($ billions)	Budget billions per Legislator	Budget billions per Staff
Defense	7	19	636.3	33.5	90.9
Labor, Health and Human Services, and Education	2	14	163.1	11.7	81.6
Veterans Affairs	3	13	76.7	5.9	25.6
Transportation, Housing, and Urban Development	2	20	67.7	3.4	33.9
Commerce, Justice, and Science	3	17	64.9	3.8	21.6
State Department	1	15	48.7	3.2	48.7
Homeland Security	3	15	42.9	2.9	14.3
Energy and Water Development	1	18	34.3	1.9	34.3
Interior and Environment	3	16	32.1	2.0	10.7
Financial Services and General Government	1	8	24.4	3.1	24.4
Agriculture	3	16	24.0	1.5	8.0
Legislative Branch	0	4	3.1	0.8	n/a

Source: Staff and legislator figures from *Roll Call*, accessed at: http://www.congressorg.org/congressorg/directory/committees.tt?commid=sappr, 13 August 2009; budget data from Senate Appropriations Subcommittee press releases summarizing FY 2010 budget, accessed at http://appropriations.senate.gov/subcommittees.cfm (13 August–20 December 2009).

priations subcommittee, it still has the largest per capita staff
workload. With seven staff members examining $636.3 billion in
spending, each staff member is responsible for about $91 billion
per year. By contrast, the median appropriations subcommittee
staff member handles just $25 billion per year, less than one-third
of the workload.

Similar workload disparities exist in the House. Most House
appropriations subcommittees have twelve members. The Defense
Subcommittee is one of three subcommittees with sixteen. Nevertheless, the per capita budget workload for legislators on the Defense Subcommittee is $39.8 billion, four times greater than the
per capita budget purview of the second-ranked Labor, Health
and Human Services, and Education Subcommittee. Although the
House in 2007 increased the Defense Subcommittee staff,[41] total
professional staff employed by the committee still numbered
fewer than two dozen.[42]

The defense budget's sheer size and complexity, compared to the
legislative and staff capabilities arrayed against it, make vigorous
oversight and coordination with authorizers difficult. Overseeing
the intelligence portion of that budget is even harder because it
constitutes less than ten percent of overall defense spending. With
$600 billion to appropriate, the Defense Subcommittee members
and their small professional staffs do not have the capacity to carefully examine the $50 billion intelligence budget. As former Senate
Intelligence Vice Chairman Kit Bond noted, the Senate Defense
Appropriations Subcommittee is overtaxed and overwhelmed.
"That committee is consumed with defense matters," said Bond.
"The committee is wrapped up in nearly a half-a-trillion-dollar
appropriations bill with less than one-tenth of it comprising the

41. SSCI, Hearing on Congressional Oversight, 110th Cong, 1st sess., 13 November 2007.

42. *Roll Call*, accessed at www.congress.org/congressorg/directory/committees.
tt?commid=happr (13 August 2009).

national intelligence program that we in the SSCI [Senate Select Committee on Intelligence] oversee." The appropriations subcommittee, Bond concluded, simply "can't give intelligence the attention it deserves." Indeed, Bond noted that the appropriations subcommittee marked up its entire Defense Department appropriation bill in "about twenty minutes," less time than the Intelligence Committee spends debating a single issue.[43] Lee Hamilton experienced the same phenomenon on the House side, noting that defense appropriators in both chambers are "mightily distracted from intelligence oversight because of their other responsibilities."[44]

Gaming the System: The Satellite Program that Would not Die. In intelligence, secrecy considerations and the enormous Defense Department budgetary workload have given rise to yawning gaps in oversight between the intelligence authorizing committees and the appropriations committees. Intelligence Committee members have complained about this problem for years. Lee Hamilton testified that when he chaired the House Intelligence Committee, he was "frequently, continually bypassed" by intelligence agencies that went instead to the appropriations committees to ensure funding of their programs.[45] Tim Roemer, who also served on the House Intelligence Committee, testified that intelligence officials "game the system," circumventing the authorizing committee that has spent months, sometimes years examining an issue by going to "two or three people on the appropriations committee."[46]

Outsiders gained a rare glimpse into this dynamic in 2004, when Senator Rockefeller, then Vice Chairman of the Senate Intelligence Committee, made public the committee's opposition to a

43. SSCI, Hearing on Congressional Oversight, 110th Cong., 1st sess., 13 November 2007.

44. Ibid.

45. Ibid.

46. Ibid.

classified satellite program on the Senate floor. The *New York Times* reported that the cost of the satellite program had ballooned from $5 billion to $9.5 billion, and that the resulting system was also so fraught with problems, it could take photographs only in daylight hours and in clear weather.[47] The faulty program was the largest single item in the intelligence budget.[48] As one official noted, "With the amount of money we're talking about here, you could build a whole new CIA."[49] Citing his "strenuous objection" to a "particular major funding acquisition program that I believe is totally unjustified and very wasteful and dangerous to national security," Senator Rockefeller noted that the Intelligence Committee had voted twice to kill the multi-billion dollar program on a bipartisan basis, but each time had been overruled by the appropriations committees.[50] Rockefeller's public comments made headlines and headaches for himself. Although the Intelligence Committee voted across party lines to kill the satellite program, Rockefeller's remarks prompted some congressional Republicans to seek a Justice Department investigation into whether the senator's floor remarks had leaked classified information and violated congressional rules. Other Republican senators considered referring the matter to the Ethics Committee.[51] Calls poured into Rockefeller's office and at least one popular radio show host accused him of illegally revealing classified secrets. The satellite program, however, was funded for three more years before finally

47. Douglas Jehl, "New Spy Plan Said to Involve Satellite System," *New York Times*, 12 December 2004.

48. Ibid.

49. Dana Priest, "New Spy Satellite Debated on Hill," *Washington Post*, 11 December 2004

50. Priest 2004. See also statement by Senator Kit Bond, SSCI Hearing 13 November 2007. It is unclear whether Bond is referring to the same satellite program that Rockefeller openly criticized or a different one.

51. David Johnston, "Justice Department May Explore Leak on Spy Satellites," *New York Times*, 15 December 2004.

being terminated by Director of National Intelligence Michael McConnell in 2007.[52]

This is not an isolated case. In 2009, a congressional intelligence staffer noted that the Senate had objected to three separate satellite programs on a bipartisan basis during the previous five years. "Two of the three have been killed," the staffer noted, "but we are still fighting over the third." When asked how long the programs were funded despite the committee's objections, the staffer replied with notable frustration, "longer than they should have been."[53] Senator John McCain grew so incensed by this pattern that in 2004 he took to the Senate floor and exhorted his colleagues to vote for his resolution granting the Intelligence Committee appropriations power. "[I]f you are the bureaucrat in Langley or at the National Security Agency or any place else, where do you go? Where do you go when you want your projects done? Do you go to the authorizing committee or do you go to the appropriations committee?" he asked rhetorically. Naturally, he said, bureaucrats go straight to the appropriators, because "the power resides in the purse." McCain concluded that "if we are going to have a truly effective Intelligence Committee oversight that can function with strength and power, we are going to have to give them appropriations authority." Otherwise, he said, the future will resemble the past. "Projects that cost a great deal of money that the Intelligence Committee either approves or disapproves of [will continue to be] overridden in the appropriations process."[54]

In sum, secrecy and budget workloads create an environment that weakens oversight by the intelligence authorizing committees.

52. Mark Mazzetti, "Spy Director Ends Program on Satellites," *New York Times*, 22 June 2007.

53. Interview by author, 20 August 2009.

54. Senator John McCain, Congressional Record p. S20634 (7 October 2004). Accessed at http://frwebgate.access.gpo.gov/cgi-bin/getpage.cgi?position=all&page=S10634&dbname=2004_record (17 July 2010).

For intelligence officials, conducting end runs around objection-
able demands by the House and Senate Intelligence Committees is
attractive. For legislators on the intelligence committees, detecting
and objecting to end runs is difficult. And for overworked appropriators who have no time to delve into the details of complicated
intelligence programs, capitulating to the end runs and granting
agency requests is often the path of least resistance.

Why Budget Reforms Fail.   Like its lack of expertise, Congress's weak budgetary hand over the Intelligence Community is
well-known, and proposals to address it have floundered. Before
9/11, the blue-ribbon Hart-Rudman Commission recommended
improving U.S. national security by, among other things, consolidating authorization and appropriations powers in the intelligence
committees.[55] After 9/11, this same proposal was the 9/11 Commission's principal recommendation for Congress. And yet since
the 2001 terrorist attacks, resolutions to grant appropriations
powers to the intelligence committees have failed three times in
the Senate and have never come before a vote in the House. Instead, the House in 2007 chose to keep appropriations powers in
the Appropriations Committee, creating a special intelligence appropriations "Select Intelligence Oversight Panel (SIOP)" that
consisted of both appropriators and intelligence committee members. Notably, the panel's recommendations were non-binding and
the arrangement was discontinued after just four years. It was re-
placed by a new system in March 2011 that allows three appropriators to attend Intelligence Committee hearings and briefings.[56]
At the time of this writing, it remains unclear just how this process

55. Hart-Rudman Commission 2001, pp. 110–113.
56. House Permanent Select Committee on Intelligence, Press Release, "Chairman
Rogers Announces Strategic Partnership with House Appropriators," 23 March
2011, accessed at http://intelligence.house.gov/sites/intelligence.house.gov/files/
documents/032311AppropriationsLiaisonsHPSCI.pdf (26 April 2011).

will work. Although it appears to be an improvement over earlier arrangements, this new system (which essentially embeds some appropriators in the Intelligence Committee to develop better knowledge of the issues and closer working relationships) still stops significantly short of moving budgetary power from the Appropriations Committee to the Intelligence Committee. The Senate has taken even less action, creating a notional Intelligence Appropriations Subcommittee in 2004 that has never actually met.[57]

Budgetary oversight reforms have failed for the same reasons the weaknesses they seek to remedy arose in the first place: The current split between authorizations and appropriations maintains Congress's internal distribution of power while at the same time serving legislators' external re-election interests.

Few things are as sacrosanct in Congress as the power of the appropriations committees. As one congressional staffer joked, "In Congress there are Democrats, Republicans, and Appropriators."[58] Political scientists have traditionally argued that appropriations committee slots are "duty" assignments that confer relatively little electoral benefit but provide members with Congress's most important internal currency: power.[59] More recent research, however, suggests that legislators gain more direct constituency benefits than previously believed. Examining district-level data and appropriations subcommittee bills from 1959 to 1998, Adler finds that half of the subcommittees are comprised of "high demanders," or members whose districts stand to gain disproportionately from the appropriations bills they consider. "Not surprisingly," he writes, "Military Construction has members from districts with high military populations or numerous military installations. . . .

57. Richard A. Best, Jr., "Intelligence Authorization Legislation: Status and Challenges," *Congressional Research Service Report* R40240, 24 February 2009; interviews with four House and Senate staff, 19–20 August 2009.

58. Interview by author, 20 August 2009.

59. Mayhew 1974.

Similarly, the Treasury, Postal Service, and General Government Subcommittee also had a number of panels that were significant outliers in terms of their districts' concern for issues involving government employees . . . ."[60] Even these duty-oriented committees, he finds, are often stacked with members who derive constituency benefits from their service.

Both forces—garnering internal power within Congress and votes outside of it—indicate that appropriators are motivated to protect their jurisdictional equities. Evidence suggests that protecting is exactly what they do. Since 9/11, only one proposal to lodge appropriations powers in the intelligence committees has ever come to a full chamber vote. It was defeated overwhelmingly in the Senate, 73–24. All but one member of the Senate Appropriations Committee voted against it. The lone appropriator who voted in favor of limiting his own committee's power, Mike DeWine (R-Ohio), actually stood to get it right back—since he also served on the Intelligence Committee. As one congressional staffer put it, "Appropriators believe in appropriations, and they are vigorous in their way of doing things and protecting their rights."[61]

SUMMARY

Congress is not designed to oversee intelligence agencies well. Since their establishment in the 1970s, the congressional intelligence committees have been conducting oversight with limited expertise and weak budgetary authority. Few, if any legislators ever have first-hand experience in the intelligence business. Despite this homegrown knowledge problem, House term limits still force members off the committee just when they have mastered

60. Adler 2002, pp. 70–71.
61. Interview by author, 20 August 2009.

the basics, making on-the-job learning a race against time. And in both chambers, legislators have not compensated for their own expertise shortfalls by bolstering staff capabilities. As intelligence agencies face proliferating threats and difficult reforms, all three routes to enhancing legislative expertise on intelligence issues have gone nowhere fast.

Congress's power of the purse also turns out to be not so powerful after all, thanks to secrecy, the budget workload, and the bifurcation of budget authority between authorizers and appropriators. Congress's budgetary system has protected the power of the appropriations committees by weakening the power of the institution as a whole, and executive branch agencies know it. Intelligence officials are not fools. In a system that invites gaming, they play to win, circumventing the intelligence committees to secure budgets from appropriators instead. So long as the intelligence committees cannot credibly threaten budgetary punishment, executive branch agencies will be less inclined to respond to their demands.

CHAPTER SIX

Conclusion

Congress's own sixty-year-old exhortation to "exercise continuous watchfulness of the execution of the administrative agencies concerned of any laws" has always been aspirational.[1] Morris S. Ogul notes in his classic examination, "No amount of congressional dedication and energy, no conceivable increase in the size of committee staffs, and no extraordinary boost in committee budgets will enable the Congress to carry out its oversight obligations in a comprehensive and systematic manner."[2] Writing in 1976, Ogul contended that this predicament applied to all policy domains. Oversight, he concluded, is destined to disappoint.

This book finds that oversight is even more likely to disappoint in intelligence than in most policy domains. Congress has always overseen other policy areas more rigorously than intelligence, for one fundamental reason: because that is where the political rewards for legislators are greater and the costs less. Intelligence is in many respects the worst of all oversight worlds: It concerns complicated policy issues that require considerable attention to

1. Legislative Reorganization Act of 1946, Public Law 601, 79th Congress, 2d sess. 2 August 1946.
2. Ogul 1976, p. 5.

master, deals with highly charged and controversial policies that are fraught with political risk, requires toiling away in secret without the promise of public prestige, and provides almost no benefit where it counts the most, at the polls. Intelligence oversight may be a vital national security issue, but it is a political loser.

The portrait of intelligence oversight painted in the preceding chapters suggests four policy implications for the future. The first is that despite all the talk of lackluster intelligence oversight during the Bush administration, congressional oversight is unlikely to improve much in the Obama administration. This is because Congress's oversight difficulties have less to do with which individuals or political parties control the White House or the congressional intelligence committees and more to do with the basic electoral incentives that drive *all* legislators to maximize their own re-election prospects. Intelligence oversight problems are so deeply rooted because they are so intimately tied to the two most valuable prizes in legislative politics: winning re-election and guarding congressional committee jurisdictions. Democrats and Republicans alike will fight to the mat for both.

The second implication stems from the first: Oversight is also unlikely to improve significantly in periods of divided government, where one party holds the presidency and the other party commands a majority in the House, the Senate, or both chambers. This may seem surprising. Political scientists have put great stock in theories of divided government when it comes to explaining political outcomes. And we know that Congress acts a lot more like "the opposition" when it is controlled by a different political party from the one sitting in 1600 Pennsylvania Avenue. One could easily imagine that a Congress controlled by one party would have powerful incentives to invest in more vigorous oversight of executive branch intelligence activities when the executive branch is run by the opposing party.

But this book finds that the story of intelligence oversight is not principally a story of party cohesion and ideological warfare waged between Democrats and Republicans running different branches of government. It is a story where all members of Congress protect congressional committee prerogatives and engage in every-man-for-himself calculations of political self-interest.

Since the CIA's creation in 1947, Americans have had forty years of divided government and twenty-six years of unified government. Yet intelligence oversight has been lackluster throughout. The post-9/11 period provides an even better view of how little divided government has mattered when it comes to improving congressional intelligence oversight capabilities. Since the terrorist attacks, the imperative for improving intelligence has been great, and the United States has experienced every possible combination of divided and unified government under different political parties. If ever there were a period in which we would expect to see dramatic improvements in intelligence oversight, the decade since 9/11 should be it. Yet this is not at all what we find.

Table 6.1 summarizes periods of divided and unified government from 2001 to the current session.

As the table illustrates, the post-9/11 period is split almost evenly between unified and divided government. From 2001 to 2003, government was divided between Republican President George W. Bush, a Republican House, and a Democratic Senate.[3] From 2003–2007, Republicans regained control of the Senate, creating unified Republican government for four years. Then the 2006 midterm elections swept Democratic majorities into both the House and Senate, returning the country to divided government for the

---

3. In May 2001, Republicans lost their razor-thin Senate majority when Senator James Jeffords of Vermont switched from Republican to Independent and decided to caucus with the Democrats.

Table 6.1 Divided and Unified Government Since 9/11

Congress	Year	President	Senate	House	Government
107th	2001–2002	R	D	R	Divided
108th	2003–2004	R	R	R	Unified
109th	2005–2006	R	R	R	Unified
110th	2007–2008	R	D	D	Divided
111th	2009–2010	D	D	D	Unified
112th	2011–2012	D	D	R	Divided

2007–2009 congressional sessions. In the 2008 presidential election, Barack Obama won the presidency and Democrats retained majorities of both chambers of Congress, creating unified government under a Democratic president from 2009 to 2011. But in the 2010 midterm elections, Democrats lost control of the House, giving rise to the first period of divided government under a Democratic president since the 9/11 attacks.

If divided government were a strong factor in strengthening intelligence oversight, we should find significant increases in oversight effectiveness and intelligence reforms during the 2001–2002, 2007–2008, and current congressional sessions. But this does not appear to be the case. While oversight "effectiveness" is always difficult to gauge, it is notable that the most sweeping intelligence reform legislation since 1947, the Intelligence Reform and Terrorism and Prevention Act, was passed (despite vigorous Pentagon opposition) in December of 2004, a period of unified government. Equally important to note is the fact that the battle lines surrounding that bill were drawn more around committee and agency jurisdictions than party affiliation. Similarly, Congress failed to pass an Intelligence Authorization Bill, which is considered the most important annual oversight legislation for the Intelligence Community, for five years in a row—between 2005

and 2010—a period that included two years of divided government and three years of unified government.[4]

I do not mean to suggest that divided government never matters.
We know that it does. My point is more narrowly targeted: Divided government does not appear to dramatically increase Congress's incentives or ability to oversee intelligence agencies as one
might expect, for all the reasons described in this book. The fact
that the most significant executive branch change in intelligence
was signed into law during a period of unified government while
authorization bills and many oversight improvements failed to
gain passage in periods of both unified and divided government
suggests that party control of all stripes—divided and unified—
probably matters less than most people think. Something larger
appears to be at work. Its name is electoral self-interest and turf
protection.

The third implication of this book is that reducing executive
branch secrecy is important but insufficient to significantly improve intelligence oversight. Improvement also requires strengthening Congress's own oversight tools. Meaningful oversight takes
two branches of government, not one. Pondering a hypothetical
example illustrates the point. Imagine for a moment a world where
no secrecy existed, where the executive branch briefed Congress
on every intelligence issue and program immediately and fully.
Would oversight improve substantially? Would agencies be held
much more accountable or work better? The answer is probably
not. For one thing, there are briefings and then there are briefings.
Briefings are only as good as the questions asked in them. Receiv-
ing nicely packaged presentations from executive branch officials
is not the same thing as vigorous probing and debate between the

4. The Democratic Congress was finally able to pass an Intelligence Authorization Bill for FY 2010, which was signed by President Obama in October.

branches. Such vigorous probing and debate does not spring naturally out of thin air. It requires legislative expertise, which takes time and effort to develop. Note here that enhancing legislative staff capabilities helps but does not suffice. When highly classified matters are being discussed, staff are not always in the room. Others have found that staff capabilities can only compensate to a certain extent.[5] Legislators themselves need to be able to ask good, hard questions to get good, tough answers. Unless Congress fosters institutional mechanisms to incentivize and develop greater expertise among members, more executive branch information will only go so far. As former Senate Majority Leader Trent Lott (R-MS) urged in 2004, "We need an Intelligence Committee whose members have years of experience in understanding the entire spectrum of global intelligence just as we have a Finance Committee whose members have spent years learning the nuances and intricacies of tax laws and Medicare."[6]

Another reason congressional oversight would probably not improve substantially in this hypothetical world is that Congress cannot demand greater bang for its intelligence buck unless and until it develops its own budgetary system to deploy resources effectively and hold agencies accountable for results. So long as the intelligence committees lack the heft to prevent budgetary end runs to appropriators, threats that agencies must "do this or else" will ring hollow and executive branch agencies will be less inclined to respond to their demands.

Major gains, in short, require Congress to reform itself. Perfect oversight is not achievable, but better oversight is. No big new ideas or even new laws are necessary. Instead, Congress should start by implementing three old ideas to change its internal operations:

5. Ogul 1976.

6. Opening remarks by Senator Trent Lott, Senate Res. 445, *Congressional Record* p. S10265, 1 October 2004. Accessed at http://frwebgate.access.gpo.gov/cgi-bin/getpage.cgi?dbname=2004_record&page=S10265&position=all (17 July 2010).

- Abolish term limits in the House Intelligence Committee
- Consolidate budgetary power in the House and Senate Intelligence Committees
- Strengthen congressional intelligence staff capabilities

These three changes certainly would not eliminate oversight problems in intelligence. But they are the most important immediate steps to mitigate them.

The fourth implication of this book is more of a cautionary warning: Do not count on these or any other major oversight improvements any time soon. This study finds that weak oversight did not arise by happenstance. Electoral self-interest on the outside and protection of turf on the inside have hindered the development of congressional intelligence expertise and weakened Congress's budgetary power for years. Inattentive voters, few and weak interest groups, and the absence of a natural district constituency make developing intelligence oversight expertise costly and unlikely. The pathologies of intelligence budgetary oversight also appear to be entrenched. Secrecy, an overburdened defense appropriations subcommittee staff, and the fragmented congressional committee system are not about to fade away. In sum, we are likely to be saddled with this oversight system for some time to come.

Ironically, the very mechanisms intended to hold legislators accountable to citizens have created an intelligence oversight system that cannot hold the executive branch accountable to Congress. Rational self-interest has led legislators across political parties, congressional committees, and historical eras to undermine Congress's collective oversight capabilities in intelligence. In the final analysis, executive branch secrecy may make meaningful intelligence oversight difficult, but Congress's self-inflicted weaknesses make it next to impossible.

ABOUT THE AUTHOR

AMY B. ZEGART is a senior fellow at the Hoover Institution and an affiliated faculty member of the Center for International Security and Cooperation at Stanford University. She was professor of public policy at the UCLA Luskin School of Public Affairs from 1999 to 2011. Zegart has been featured by *The National Journal* as one of the ten most influential experts in intelligence reform. Her research includes two award-winning books—*Spying Blind: The CIA, the FBI, and the Origins of 9/11* and *Flawed by Design: The Evolution of the CIA, JCS, and NSC*. She was a member of The National Academies of Science Panel to Improve Intelligence Analysis, and serves on the Federal Bureau of Investigation Intelligence Analysts Association National Advisory Board and the Los Angeles Police Department's Counterterrorism and Community Police Advisory Board.

About the Hoover Institution's

KORET-TAUBE TASK FORCE

ON NATIONAL SECURITY AND LAW

The KORET-TAUBE TASK FORCE ON NATIONAL SECURITY AND LAW examines the rule of law, the laws of war, and American constitutional law with a view to making proposals that strike an optimal balance between individual freedom and the vigorous defense of the nation against terrorists both abroad and at home. The task force's focus is the rule of law and its role in Western civilization, as well as the roles of international law and organizations, the laws of war, and U.S. criminal law. Those goals will be accomplished by systematically studying the constellation of issues—social, economic, and political—on which striking a balance depends.

Current members of the Koret-Taube Task Force on National Security and Law are: Kenneth Anderson, Peter Berkowitz (chair), Philip Bobbit, Jack Goldsmith, Stephen D. Krasner, Jessica Stern, Matthew Waxman, Ruth Wedgwood, and Benjamin Wittes.

INDEX